Rose Blanche: Keeping the Past Alive

George Rose

Somewhat Grumpy Press

This book is a memoir. It provides the author's recollections of experiences, events, and conversations over time. Some names and characteristics have been changed, some events have been compressed or re-arranged for story purposes, and some dialogue has been recreated. The content reflects historical attitudes and opinions.

Any public figures, institutions, trade names or organizations that may be pictured or mentioned in the book have not endorsed this book, have not made any payment for mention, and are not otherwise associated with the book, author, or publisher. No generative artificial intelligence was used in preparing this work.

Published by arrangement with Somewhat Grumpy Press Inc. Halifax, Nova Scotia, Canada. SomewhatGrumpyPress.com The Somewhat Grumpy Press name and Pallas' cat logo are registered trademarks.

ISBN 978-1-998555-04-8 (paperback)
ISBN 978-1-998555-05-5 (eBook)

Originally published 2019. This edition is revised and expanded, with new photos.

January 2025 v4

Contents

This book is dedicated to my late wife,
Effie Marina Rose (née Way),
who gave me a beautiful life and four wonderful daughters,
Connie, Carol, Cathy, and Cindy.

Chapter One

Keeping the Past Alive

I have been very fortunate to keep alive my past. My wonderful children, and especially my eight grandchildren, have helped me tremendously to relive my early life, growing up in Rose Blanche. To be nostalgic, I believe, is not a sin. I love not only to relive the moments of my youth in my mind, but I also love to pass it on to my grandchildren and to anyone else who might be interested in what my grandchildren call "the olden days."

As far as I can see, those precious moments have already almost completely disappeared and I think it's a shame that we don't make an effort to at least record those days even though, not in our wildest dreams, would we want to relive them. These days, I am living in a retirement home in Nova Scotia. I have plenty of time to sit back and revisit the days of my youth, especially the growing-up years in the 1930s and 1940s. Most of these memories are very dear to me and any day when I can dwell on them, even for a short time, I certainly don't think it's time wasted.

This work is not meant to glorify the past. Rather it is an honest attempt to show what it was like almost a hundred years ago, how we coped with what was happening then in Rose Blanche. We can't live in the past and I would never want to see a resurrection of the way of life we had back then. But if we read about the past, it can help us see where we came from and understand the present—show we got to where we are today. Sometimes nostalgia is unpleasant and serves no useful purpose, but there are so many things in my past, growing up in Rose Blanche, that are worth remembering and which I still cherish.

I have tried to accurately depict the years that I spent there as a child. Rose Blanche has a place in my memory that time has not diminished or erased, and I hope and expect it never will. Going back there, even now after so many years, does something to me that no other place that I lived in can do. When I visited Rose Blanche in 2016, I expected it to be my last visit home. In my closing remarks, as master of ceremony for the Come Home Year celebration I included these words:

"When I dip down the hill over there near the post office and stop at the church parking lot and I see the panoramic view of Rose Blanche spread out before me I get what my mother used to call the 'cold shivers' and I'm covered with goose bumps. I love beyond words the rugged beauty of this place and when I reach that spot, near the church, it feels like I've come to a place which is very, very special. And it's then I realize—I'm in Rose Blanche—I have come home!!! This beautiful place is my birthplace—where I was born and grew up."

I always consider myself fortunate enough to have lived my dream there. I will never forget that I grew up in a great community, with loving parents, excellent friends, and so many thoughtful and caring neighbours. It has been at the urging of my late wife and my four daughters that I have written this book, to record and share that joy.

In this book, I recall, relive, and record "The WAY IT WAS" when I grew up in this wonderful place. I do hope you may enjoy reading it as much as I enjoyed writing it.

George Rose.

Telling Stories

My wife and I always thought our family was the most important part of our lives. For many years, after I retired, we would leave our home in Newfoundland to spend the winter with our daughters and grandchildren in Nova Scotia. We always wanted to be there and be part of their growing up.

Whenever I visited, my grandchildren would want poppy to tell them bedtime stories. I would always ask them what they would like to hear and invariably they would say "tell us what it was like when you were growing up in Rose Blanche in the olden days."

They seemed fascinated about how a person could exist without TV, computers, or the phones that play such an integral part in their young lives today. They wanted to know the way people lived, did things, and how they played and spent their time. "Weren't you bored, poppy, in those olden times with nothing to play with?"

I have never regretted one solitary minute of my growing up in Rose Blanche. I enjoyed telling them how we did things, how we spent our time and, believe it or not, I was never bored. To them it seemed almost impossible one could live under these conditions in an isolated place and enjoy it. And enjoy it I did. Recalling these memories, I could close my eyes while I was talking to them and relive many of the incidents they wanted to hear. They listened attentively, but I could tell by the looks on their precious faces they had a hard time absorbing my answers.

Many of the things we did, which are described in this book, may not seem exciting to people today. But I have always believed that a very important part of our character is shaped by events and things that have gone on before in our lives. My children and grandchildren know me by my stories.

Chapter Two

Welcome to Rose Blanche

R ose Blanche has a rugged beauty that makes it one of the most picturesque communities in Eastern Canada. It is on the southeast coast of Newfoundland, eighteen miles east of the western terminus town of Port aux Basques, home of the ferry that operates between there and North Sydney in Nova Scotia.

Origins

The name Rose Blanche was probably derived from the French words "roche blanche," because of the white quartz visible throughout the area. The deposits in Diamond Cove can be seen when viewed from out to sea and was probably used by the French fishermen, active in the area in the 1700s, as a navigational aid.

The white rocks of Diamond Cove.

The harbour itself is surrounded by high land and is considered a safe anchorage. It is protected on the east side by a small peninsula called The Neck. On the south is Caines Island. Larger islands, Duck and Hopkin's, to the west, protect the harbour from the fierce Atlantic swells. And on the north side are the high hills on the sides of which the settlement of Rose Blanche was built.

Rose Blanche Harbour as seen from the town.

Crow Cove

There are three deep inlets in the harbour itself. Crow Cove is on the west side.

Big Bottom

Big bottom is on the east side.

These three inlets are divided by two points of land jutting out into the harbour, Parson's Point and Misery Point.

Parson's Point

Misery Point

Between the two is Lennies Harbour.

Lennies Harbour

Many place names in the area bear witness to the French fishermen, including Harbour La Cou, Braziel, and Petites. The famous British explorer Captain James Cook, who was mapping the west coast of Newfoundland, visited Rose Blanche in 1759. He commented on what a safe and snug harbour it was. He wrote in his log that no one lived in Rose Blanche proper. Cook recorded that there was one fishing stage in Harbour La Cou, but he failed to name the family.

Harbour Le Cou

It wasn't until 1810 that three families came to live in Rose Blanche. These were the Caines, Currie, and Paynes, and they built their homes on Caines Island to be as close as possible to the fishing grounds.

In those days the inners harbours of Big Bottom, Crow Cove, and Lennies Harbour froze over during the winters, and being on the island at the mouth of the harbour meant they had access to the fishing grounds while the inner harbour was still blocked with ice.

Caines Island

In the 1840 census, two other families, the Buffets and Roses, were added to the list. These were people from Hermitage and Placentia Bay. Later, men who fished in Burgeo and farther down the coast immigrated to Rose Blanche. Many of these people had previously been sponsored by the Jersey merchants who had a plantation headquarters located in Harbour Breton on the south coast. As the fishing grounds became overcrowded in this area, the fishermen moved up the coast towards Rose Blanche. By the late 1840s, the community had grown, and people moved from the outer perimeter to the inner harbour; especially the Roses, who moved to Misery Point.

In the late 1840s, the Reverent William Marshal visited the area and met with a man called Brown from Bay La Moine. During this trip, he married the daughter of Francis Payne to Richard Sweet. Marshal was amazed at the fondness and ability of the inhabitants for dancing. I can attest to the fact that this had not changed one iota when I was growing up.

Growth of the Fishing Industry

Fish flake

Early fishing took place mainly in the spring and summer. Some boats fished near St. Paul's Island in the Cabot Strait while others went to the coastal areas in Labrador. They salted their catch aboard their boats and returned when loaded to cure their salt bulk catch on the many fish flakes constructed around the community. September was the best month to dry the fish for export as the sun in September was not so direct and would not sunburn the fish.

By 1870, Rose Blanche was flourishing fishing community with two large merchants, namely Benjamin Smith and Philip Sorsolii, as well as a clergyman and a doctor. Vessels from Nova Scotia and Massachusetts were trading and fishing in the area. The Americans were more interested herring than cod.

The town grew during the 1870s with development of a winter fishery based on cod. Back in 1850, Captain Henry Smith, of Gloucester, Massachusetts, was the first to attempt a large scale winter fishery in Rose Blanche, focusing on frozen herring. The man credited establishing the winter fishery was Thomas Ridley from Harbour Grace. He had a business in Rose Blanche that was managed by Thomas Le Sellevies.

The gulf stream flowing up the Eastern Atlantic seaboard touches the southwest coast of Newfoundland just west of Rose Blanche. As a result, the ice in the Gulf of St. Lawrence seldom reached as far east along the coast as this section of the island. In the winter, large schools of cod fish migrate down ahead of the ice floe and spread over the area known locally as the Rose Blanche Banks. Despite the weather, the winter fishery was lucrative.

With the introduction of the winter fishery, men stayed longer on the fishing banks and returned later in the day. By the time they set out for port, it was too dark to see the white rocks of Diamond Cove to guide them back home. There was a pressing need for some other navigational aid. A petition was written, signed, and presented to the house of assembly in St. John's, asking for a light house to be built on the coast.

An engineer, Mr. Neville, was sent to the area and he recommended that a light house be built on a piece of land called The Neck in Rose Blanche. The construction started in 1871. The light house was built of granite. Oxen were used to bring stones to the site, where masons cut and shaped it. The light apparatus was designed and constructed by the Stevenson engineering firm in Edinburgh in Scotland. It was installed in 1873.

Rose Blanche Lighthouse

Fog alarm

A few decades later, the light house was complemented by a fog alarm and light that was built on Caines Island, just a short distance from Rose Blanche Point.

After decades of storms, the Rose Blanche lighthouse largely collapsed in 1957, though the tower and light remained in use until the 1980s.

The Rose Blanche lighthouse was restored in the 1990s, by local workers, using stones from the original structure and supplemented by stones from the original quarry site. The beam from this light can be seen fifteen miles out to sea. This is the only working granite light house in Atlantic Canada and today is a registered heritage structure and quite a tourist treasure for Rose Blanche.

Rose Blanche Lighthouse. Photo by Cathy Rose.

The 1870s winter fishery meant processing work for Thomas Ridley's firm, as well as Robert Moulton's firm from Burgeo, and Harvey and Company's from St. John's. The latter company pioneered the fresh fish filleting and cold storage system in 1915. The freezing and storage of the fish was carried out on board a three-mast schooner called the *Sunset Glow* which spent each winter fishing season in Rose Blanche. A dense brine solution was used to freeze the fillets before storage below the deck. Periodically a smaller ship would take the frozen fillets to the American market.

During the 1860s and 1870s, some of the men who fished in the summer on the Labrador coast left Rose Blanche and helped pioneer settlements in the Bonne Bay area, on the west coast. Many of the family names so common in Rose Blanche are no longer present, such as Ellsworths, Paynes, Pittmans, and Shears. These names were replaced by a series of new names such as the Billards from Grand Bruit, Farrells from North Bay, Herrits and Strouds from Baker's Tickles, Pinks and Keepings from Cape La Hune and Burnt Islands, Stricklands from West Point and Burgeo, Macdonalds and Spencers from Cul De Sac, and Durnfords from Francois.

The Moulton business went bankrupt in the early 1900s. Luke Chafe, from Petty Harbour, prospered for a few years in the early 1930s, during the depression, but later left the area. In 1930, a business owned by Wilson Horwood and situated at the very end of Misery Point caught fire and was completely destroyed. He and his family left Rose Blanche to take up residence in St. John's where he established a thriving family business.

The Fishing Industry I Knew

In the 1930s and 1940s, when I was growing up, Rose Blanche, like many years before, was the centre for the winter fishery on the southwest coast of Newfoundland. In Rose Blanche, Diamond Cove, and Harbour Le Cou, there were approximately fifty-five fishing vessels. These were one and two dory fishing boats called "skiffs" by the local people. They were in reality small schooners, ranging from fifteen to twenty-five tons. Many of these boats were built in North Bay, Lapoile, by the Farrells and Stricklands.

Fishing skiff. Photo by Lydia Collier.

In February, these boats were complemented by the Grand Bank fishing schooners, which would appear to take part in this lucrative winter fishery. These schooners did not sell their fish to the processing plants. The fish was cleaned and salted on board, usually late in the evening when they returned to port.

The harbour looked like a small town itself, with many lanterns hung in the schooners' riggings while they processed and stored their catch. In the days, and there were many in the winter, when it was not suitable for fishing, the local roads and shops were crowded with fishermen from the schooners who came ashore to have a much needed break from their quarters on board. Boats from as far away as Francois appeared and found anchorage in the inner harbour.

There were three fish plants in Rose Blanche, and each worked to capacity during the winter fishing season: Seafoods from Halifax, Harvey and Company from St. John's, and Leonard Brothers from North Sydney. They all processed fresh fish for the American market.

Seafoods and Leonards both had bunkhouses attached to their plants to accommodate men from as far away as Fortune Bay who came to work on the fish plants. Most local men were engaged in the fishery so there was a shortage of labourers. A few women were employed to pack the fish fillets in ice. The price of fish in those days wasn't very high—cod fetched three cents a pound, haddock four cents, and ocean perch was worth a penny a pound. Fish in those days were plentiful. There were times when the fishermen had to stay ashore because the plants had so much fish it took several days to process it all. What a contrast to present times!

The economy of Rose Blanche prior to, during, and long after the 1930s and 1940s was based entirely on the fishery. There was no other economic activity and except for a few positions, like clerks in general stores, for most people there was no other way of making a living. The fishing for cod kept the place active and, to a certain extent, prosperous.

A Fishing Season

The fishing industry had an annual cycle. The most important day of the fishing year was May 1st. On that day, men shifted from one boat's crew to another to remain there for the coming year. By then, fish had left the Rose Blanche Banks and fishing there was no longer profitable. On that day there was a feeling of freedom in the air and the oft-uttered adage was heard: "today Jack is as good as his master." There would be celebrating, much liquor consumed and in a few cases the parting of a crew member from his past year's captain was not done very benevolently.

On the next day, preparations would be made for the summer fishery. Men would clean and paint their boats and stock the galleys. Shortly after, the boats would leave for Nova Scotia where they would fish and sell their fresh catch to fish plants in Glace Bay/Ingonish area. The men lived aboard their boats. They fished there until near the end of June. By that time, they would have earned enough money to go to North Sydney and load their boats with coal to last the year to heat the house and to cook with.

Smaller skiffs of near ten tons would have a crew of four men and each crew member would probably get three tons of coal from the June trip. Larger boats had a six men crew and could carry a larger load but that first trip in June resulted in each man getting about the same amount. The coal would be unloaded and placed near the wharf. Then the onerous task of carrying it to the shed or store house was left to the women and young ones, who for several days would be as busy as bees.

Then the boats were cleaned and fitted to go sword fishing off the coast of Nova Scotia. To do this, the boat had to be fitted with a foretop and a sword fish chair. An iron contraption called a chair was fastened to the end of the bowsprit. Surrounded by the iron protection, the harpooner could sit there and await his chance to harpoon the swordfish. The foretop was an approximately twenty-foot extension that was attached to the fore mast. It usually had padded iron hoops with a suspended seat in each. From there the men could have an extended view of the sea and could see a swordfish at a great distance from the boat. A steering wheel was connected by rope to the tiller on the stern of the boat.

When a swordfish was seen basking on the surface, the man seated on the foretop would take control of the boat and from his perch he would be able to manoeuvre the boat so the harpooner could get the best shot at the fish. When the fish was harpooned, a dory would be launched from the boat and a man would take control and tire out the fish and bring it to the surface.

Swordfishing was a lucrative fishery that lasted from early July until September, when the swordfish left the area. The average swordfish weighed in excess of three hundred pounds and was sold at a very high price. Most boats would harvest in the twenties with an occasional boat in the thirties.

When this fishery ended in September, the boats went again to North Sydney to get loaded with coal. Any excess money would be spent on purchasing clothing, flour, sugar, and other items. At that time Newfoundland was not a province of Canada and these goods were much cheaper in Nova Scotia. If purchased openly they would be subject to a tariff of upwards to forty percent on the price. Thus, the boats would time their arrival back home to Rose Blanche at night so that these goods could be smuggled ashore and put away before the local custom officer would arrive in the morning to search and "clear" the boat.

The second load of coal was unloaded and now each crew member had enough coal to last the year. If from the larger boats there was any excess, it would be sold to the schools, church or to a few families who had no men on the boats. A ton of coal in those days was sold for around ten dollars.

With the last load of coal landed and stored for the winter the boats, after being cleaned, went to the bay down the coast for a load of wood since there were no trees near Rose Blanche. Wood was needed to provide a supply of kindling to start the coal fire each morning. At this time, they would also get the trees that were needed to keep their wharves, stages, and sheds in good repair. Some crews might be lucky enough to bag a caribou or a moose.

Upon returning home the men unloaded the trees, and removed the bark so they would dry quicker. Kindling, small portions split off from a junk of wood, would be brought into the house each evening and sometimes placed in the oven to dry. Later in the evening, the man of the house would remove the kindling and use his pocketknife to make shavings, then place them underneath the stove, ready to start the fire in the morning. At our house, when we saw Dad rise from the kitchen couch and open his pocketknife, we knew it was time to get ready for bed.

For the rest of September and October, the men were very busy. Wharves had to be repaired and stages made ready for the winter fishery. Others would be painting their houses and storehouses or sheds, and fixing up the bridges and things around the house. A few extra dollars might be made by some men from a grant, given each year from the government, to repair the roads in the community.

The biggest task was for fishermen was getting their gear ready for the coming winter fishery. I remember the not unpleasant odour of tar that permeated the house when Dad cut and tied the gingins (a yard long line to hold the fishhook). These gingins, sometimes called suds, were attached to the trawl lines. A trawl line was an eighteen pound hemp line. Eight of these lines made up a tub of gear.

Fishermen would try to get in extra days of early fishing, to amass a few extra dollars to make the coming festive season a bit more enjoyable. But usually, the weather in late November and early December was unsettled and blustery and they would be very lucky to get in three or four days fishing. And since the large quantities of fish had not yet arrived on the Rose Blanche Banks, their catches were very light.

In January the gulf began to freeze over, and the cod started to migrate in large numbers towards the southwest coast of the island. The weather settled and the fishing began in earnest. The fish were now plentiful, and the boats would make large catches.

Fishing for cod, far out to sea in the middle of winter, was not a job for the faint hearted. Men left for the fishing grounds before dawn on a suitable day. They steamed to the banks about ten to twelve miles offshore. On arrival, the skiff would drop off her one or two dories with two men aboard each. The men would set the trawl that they had baited in their stages the night before. They would usually set four tubs of trawl. One man rowed the dory with the flow of the tide which ran towards the east or west depending on the rising or falling of the tides, while the other set out the trawl. In the meantime, the skipper would keep the skiff fairly close to the dories while having a sharp lookout on the weather conditions. When the trawl had been set, the dories would return to the skiff and have a lunch while they waited for the trawl to fish.

After several hours, the men would return to the trawls and begin to retrieve them. One man would pull the trawl up, from about one hundred fathoms, unhook the fish while the other man stood well behind him, helping him to pull up the trawl and at the same time coiling it in the trawl tubs (which were actually half barrels). When the dory had a fair quantity of fish, the men would raise an oar and the mother boat would come along side. The fish would be forked up on board with a pitchfork called a prong.

If the fish were plentiful, as the men continued to haul the trawl, the captain and the extra crew member would bait extra tubs of trawl with the usual herring or squid bits and be prepared to set additional trawls later.

Most boats returned to port before dusk, cleaning the catch on the way in. But there were times in those days when the fish were so plentiful that the boats just couldn't leave the fishing grounds until it was dark. I can still remember one boat coming into port well after dark with a load of fish that weighed in at twenty-eight thousand pounds. This could occur quite often. However, the average catch per day for a one dory boat would be around ten thousand pounds and for a two dory boat usually in the very high teens.

When finished weighing their fish at the fish plant and after a quick supper at home, the men returned to their respective stages and baited the trawl that had to be ready for the next morning. This usually meant working long into the night.

The quality of the fish caught during the winter was high. Only hook and line fishing was used and the fish, when caught, were on deck in the open air usually near or below freezing. The fish would be processed at the fish plant the same day it arrived.

In several consecutive fishing days, the boats would catch enough fish that the three fish plants, working from eight in the morning to eleven at night, could not accept any more fish from the boats. Later returning boats would have to sell their catch to either Newman Brothers or Harvey Company who would have it split, salted, and later in the summer have it sun dried on the fish flakes.

One summer, I was hired to pick up the small fish that fell through the spaces on the fish flakes. I was eleven, but I don't recall any laws regarding child labour in those days. I wasn't paid any money, but the store manager gave me two grey flannel shirts from his store's stock, which I proudly wore that winter.

Most of the boats had crews of four men, called one dory boats, or six men with two dories. One-fifth of the daily catch went towards the boat expenses and the other four-fifths were evenly divided among the crew. Each man received what was called a full share.

In some cases, a man would serve as what was called a "shareman." This, usually a young person, would not have to buy fishing supplies and lived and ate at the captain's house. He was expected to do most of the house chores, and he received a half of a full share of the allotted catch. Other boats sometimes carried an extra man not counted as part of the crew. He would have four lines of his own gear attached to the boats trawl and all the fish on these four lines were for him alone. Of course, he helped with all other tasks associated with the boat.

Fishing in small boats in the wintertime ten or twelve miles from shore was often at times a precarious occupation, to say the least. Sometimes storms would suddenly arise, like the disastrous storm of 1925 where eighteen fishermen lost their lives in three fishing boats that never made it back to port. Sometimes a storm would come on so quickly that they would have to leave their trawls and hurry back to port before the storm got worse. At times like these, men would be kept busy beating ice from the riggings and the other parts of the boat, formed from the sea spray, before the ice changed the centre of gravity of the boat and caused it to capsize.

To fish under winter conditions, the fishermen had to be very cognizant of the weather conditions and be able to predict what the weather would be like. Not many men trusted the forecasts from the radio because they seemed to be too general. The men depended on other weather signs. They became experts by watching the clouds and their shape, height and drift, the moon with its haze and, most important of all, the rise and fall of the barometer.

There was one large barometer on display in the post office window. Before dusk each night, most men would be sure to have a good look at it. My father had his own barometer, or weather glass, and from it he could predict the weather, such as winds and rain, by how fast the needle moved and where it pointed. Almost every night we would have a number of visitors asking what the weather was going to be like the next day. My dad's predictions almost always seemed to be more accurate that the forecast from the radio.

By March and April, many boats fished in the day and, before they left the fishing grounds, they would set several tubs of gear to fish overnight and pick up the next day. These were referred to as "night sets."

Men in Rose Blanche never fished on Sundays. This was their day of rest. The only time a boat went out on Sunday was to try and retrieve a string of expensive gear that the men were forced to leave a day or so before, because of a storm.

Near the end of April, with the fish getting scarcer day by day, the winter fishery came to a close. The year's cycle was now complete, and the preparations began for the next season, under the warmer spring weather.

Decline of the Fishery

After World War Two, demand for salted cod, on which at that time the industry in Newfoundland largely depended, slowly began to disappear. This was partly due to reduced observance of meatless Fridays in Catholic countries such as Spain, Portugal, and Italy, and among Catholic populations in Canada and the United States, made official by statements of various church authorities in the 1960s. Meanwhile, improvements in fishing, shipping and transportation led to Iceland and Norway becoming larger suppliers of salted cod.

This led to the demise of the large Grand Bank fishing fleet which supplied their European markets with this salt cod. The numerous fish flakes in Rose Blanche, on both sides of Lennies Harbour, used to dry the salt cod, began to deteriorate and have now all disappeared.

During the same time, the value of fresh fish increased when dieticians began to herald the benefits of fish in our diets, and improvements in shipping and transportation made getting fresh fish to distant markets more feasible. The market for fresh fish expanded greatly. The fishing industry in Rose Blanche switched from salted to fresh fish to supply the American markets. However, worldwide demand for fresh fish ended the cod fishery in Rose Blanche.

Large factory ships, each with their flotilla of draggers, began to appear off Rose Blanche when the winter fishery was at its height. The factory ships, from Russia, Spain, and Portugal, processed their fish at sea. Their large draggers not only dragged the fish on the Rose Blanche Banks, but their heavy nets tore up the sea bottom and destroyed the biomass that the fish fed on. It was plowed up beyond repair. There was nothing left for the few remaining fish to eat. At night, these large ships and their draggers came close to shore, well inside the then three mile limit of territorial waters. Again, they dragged the ocean bottom, cleaning it of fish and making it impossible for most living things to even exist there.

It is so disappointing to see the once prosperous and thriving community of Rose Blanche that I grew up in reduced to a retirement settlement and a place where some people spend their summers, away from the heat and pollution of mainland cities. The population has decreased to a little over one-third of what it used to be. There are no longer any jobs in the fishing industry there. The hardy Rose Blanche fishermen left to earn a living elsewhere, mostly on the mainland. The four schools are all closed, since there are no longer any young families living there to provide children to keep them open.

In 2006, I had the opportunity to be Master of Ceremonies for the Come Home Year celebrations in Rose Blanche. One of my duties was to "screech in" several mainlanders who wanted to be honorary Newfoundlanders. In one part of the ceremony, the participants were supposed to kiss a cod. I was amazed to find out there wasn't a cod fish to be found anywhere in Rose Blanche. Rose Blanche was founded on the cod fish, and had been the only reason for its existence as a community. How times changed.

Confederation

In Rose Blanche, in the 1930s and 1940s, we operated under the credit system. We had a little black book which we took with us when we went to the general store. We'd purchase essentials like kerosene, molasses, sugar, tea, and salt beef and port, and the item purchased would be entered into the large ledger kept at the store, and also into our little black book. Later, when Dad returned from sword fishing or when the winter fishery season was over, he would pay his debts, or settle up. Like many fishermen, there was very little left over after the debts were paid.

Anything we needed besides the essentials, especially clothing, would be ordered from the Eaton's or Simpson's catalogues before these tomes were recycled to the outhouse. A lot of clothes were smuggled in from Nova Scotia by the men when they fished there, since anything purchased from the catalogues was subject to a forty per cent tariff. In the late 1940s, Joe Smallwood got lots of votes from Rose Blanche when, among other things, he promised that the tariff would disappear if Newfoundland became a province of Canada.

In the late 1800s, Newfoundland was a prosperous and self-governed dominion. It had rejected joining the Dominion of Canada in 1867. However, several disasters and unwise government decisions forced it to eventually give up its government.

In 1892, Newfoundland's two banks collapsed and went out of business. In 1894, a large fire destroyed almost all of St. John's. At about the same time, the government began borrowing money to finance a railway across the country with the hope it would open up the interior of the island for development. This led to the paper mill at Grand Falls and the opening of a mine at Buchans. The railway, however, became a big drain on the government and never made a profit.

In 1914, the First World War broke out and Newfoundland was the first dominion to answer Britain's call for help. The Newfoundland government borrowed money to finance an army that served throughout the war. She offered more enlistments and had the most casualties per capital of any dominion. Her army did her proud. It became the first and only army that had the word royal added to its name while still fighting. Among its many battle honours, it had the youngest soldier ever to receive the Victoria Cross in a combat role—Sargent Tommy Ricketts, at age sixteen. Several battles, especially at Beaumont Hamel in 1916, almost wiped out the regiment and Newfoundland lost most of a generation of her best young men that day.

When the depression struck in 1929, Newfoundland was in deep trouble. She had also borrowed money to pay her war debt, the only dominion to fully do so, and now she was so far in debt she couldn't even pay the interest on it. The government asked Canada for help, but Canada was having troubles of its own. When Newfoundland turned to the mother country for help, the British government sent Lord Amulre with a group to find out what was wrong and to suggest a way to correct it. Amulre recommended that, because of the large debt and corruption in the government, the dominion should suspend its present form of government and be ruled by a commission: six men, three from Britain and three from Newfoundland. At the head was to be a governor appointed by the British parliament. The commission was given the task of paying off the island's debt and then responsible government would be restored.

The economy of Newfoundland improved somewhat with the coming of the Second World War, and the building of United States bases along with an influx of U.S. servicemen. However, the commission's main concern was the debt, and the infrastructure of Newfoundland was neglected and allowed to deteriorate.

In 1946, Great Britain was in economic straits due to the tremendous cost of the Second World War. She began to divest herself of much of her vast empire, much of which was at the same time clamouring for independence. Newfoundland was a small problem that could easily be gotten rid of. Waiting in the wings was Canada, who considered Newfoundland's position then as a fortress guarding the entrance to the mighty St. Lawrence which led to the very heart of the North American hinterland. Its possession would completely flesh out Sir John A's vison of what Canada should be.

By then, the commission of government had successfully fulfilled its mandate. Newfoundland's debts were paid and there was a surplus of fifty millions dollars in the bank. Thus, in 1946, a convention was held, in St. John's, with delegates from all over the island, to choose between returning to dominion status with responsible government as promised in 1934, or continuing government by commission.

A pig farmer at the convention, named Joe Smallwood, from Gambo, convinced the convention that it should also consider the option of confederation with Canada. After much furious debate, Joey, as he was to be affectionally called by many Newfoundlanders, with the help of much pressure from Britain and financial help from Canada, managed to get that option put on the ballet of June 1948. In that election, neither responsible government, commission government, nor confederation received a majority. Commission Government was then dropped from the next ballot and in August 1948, confederation with Canada received a very narrow majority and on March 31, 1949, Newfoundland became Canada's tenth province.

In Rose Blanche, like most rural area, there was no question how the vote would go. I remember an old lady near where I lived who received a widow's pension of ten dollars every three months. Joey said that each pensioner, under confederation, would receive forty dollars every month. No one had to wonder what she would vote for.

Similar promises of family allowances for each child, elimination of the tariffs on clothing and other good from Nova Scotia, and a whole lot of other financial benefits won the votes of many people not only in Rose Blanche but from many of the other outports around the island.

Those who favoured responsible government were using arguments of honour, loyalty to the past our fathers fought for, and other such philosophical reasons why one should vote for them. Though all Newfoundlanders were very proud of what their forefathers had accomplished, those arguments didn't put food on the table. When it came time to vote, the practical needs of the stomach overcame the philosophical yearnings of the heart.

There were other incentives to vote for confederation. In Rose Blanche, the fishermen spent months fishing in Nova Scotia, and brought back tales of the differences in the infrastructure there compared to at home. When the confederates promised that Canada would bring Newfoundland up to the same standard as the Maritime provinces, there was little doubt what the people in Rose Blanche would vote for. And many of the older people remembered what conditions were like in the early 1930s when they suffered under the so-called responsible government. Few outside the Avalon Peninsula wanted to see it return.

Sir John A. must still be smiling to see his dream completed.

Chapter Three

Celebrity Connections

A lthough Rose Blanche was and still is a small and isolated, seemingly unimportant community, it has been touched by several very famous people.

Captain James Cook

As already noted in the history, an early visitor to the area, before there was a community, was the famous English explorer Captain James Cook. He visited Rose Blanche in 1759. He noted that Rose Blanche had an excellent anchorage. Over five seasons, he mapped the coasts of Newfoundland, with such accuracy that the maps were used for navigation for over a hundred years. He also mapped the mouth of the St. Lawrence River. His achievements in Newfoundland led to his three Pacific Expeditions, where he mapped the coast of British Columbia, searched for the western entrance to the Northwest passage, and travelled to such far-flung destinations as Tahiti, Easter Island, Australia, and New Zealand.

Robert Louis Stevenson

Another famous person connected to Rose Blanche was the noted English author Robert Louis Stevenson. In the summer of 1873, he was home from his studies at Oxford University, and spent that summer working in his father's engineering firm. He no doubt had a hand in building the light apparatus for the Rose Blanche light house. He went on to write the famous novels *Treasure Island* and *Kidnapped* as well as a children's book of poetry.

Zane Grey

American author Zane Grey knew Rose Blanche. He is widely recognized as the Father of the American Western novel. He wrote not only westerns but also other well-known books about sports, especially fishing. Many of his records of fish trophies, especially caught on light tackle, still stand today. In the late 1920s he spent several summers in Rose Blanche as a guest of Wilson Horwood's. The two of them together fished for salmon in Garia Bay river.

Cassie Brown

Cassier Brown was the daughter of Wilson Horwood, and she was born on Misery Point. She spent the first twelve years of her young life there. At the age of twelve, she and her friend, a boy named Billy Rolls, decided to stow away in a locker on a schooner which had just left Rose Blanche with a load of dried fish, headed for Portugal. Just outside the harbour, they were discovered and returned to Rose Blanche.

She moved to St. John's and became a very well-known writer and newspaper personality there. But she is most famous for the several books she wrote narrating sea disasters in Newfoundland. The book that brought her world fame was her masterpiece, *Death on the Ice*, describing the disaster that occurred in 1914 when a whole ship's sealing crew was caught on the ice in a storm and every man perished. Among her other books is *Stand into Danger*, the story of the three American ships, *Wilkes*, *Pollux* and *Trustum*, which ran ashore with much loss of life on the shore near Lawn and St. Lawrence on the Burin peninsula.

Chapter Four

My Family

I have always considered myself very fortunate to have two such loving people as my parents. My father and mother gave me a strong moral base on which I could call on whenever I had to make an important decision and I have always tried to live up to their expectations. Although they both have long departed this life, I still find myself constantly referring to their teachings whenever I have to decide something really important. I often wonder what they would think of some of the decisions that I have made. What a precious gift that two parents could give to their child! I hope and pray that I have been as successful in passing on to my children the strong moral base I got, to guide them when needed.

My dad was away fishing or working for almost half the year so, Mom was the dominant parent in our family. She took care of us and the home during his absence. She was continuously at work, but we never felt neglected. She was stern, but loving and kind, and showered us with oodles of her motherly love.

A Remarkable Woman

Under Mom's tutelage, truth took up permanent residence in our home, and respect and integrity became its roommates. Even when Dad was home, he deferred to Mom in almost everything pertaining to us or the household. In Mom's domain there was no room for rumour, gossip, or innuendo, and accusations needed to be accompanied by unimpeachable evidence. We were taught to respect our elders, calling them aunt or uncle though they were no kin to us. I was told to tip my cap whenever I met the minister on the road, and we always referred to people like the managers of the local businesses as Mister.

Mom was born in East Bay, Lapoile, being one of twelve children in her family. Since there were only four families in East Bay, there was no school. Mom never had a chance to go to school so she could neither read nor write but she was so intelligent that none of us for a minute ever thought she needed either of the two. We never even thought to teach her.

Mom left East Bay at age sixteen and came to Rose Blanche, to work as a servant girl for a large family. Later, she moved to North Sydney, Nova Scotia, doing the same thing there. In 1928 she married Dad. In the next eight years became the mother of two boys and two girls.

Mom had many talents. She could take an old potato sack and, with strips from worn out clothes, hook mats that were placed near our beds and at the entrance to our house. She cleaned, carded, and spun wool into yarn to knit our socks, mitts, and sweaters. She had a table model Singer sewing machine and with it she could make and alter my sister's clothes. She was a specialist in making the thick quilts, heirlooms now, for all our beds.

Her meals, cookies, cakes, and pies were exceptional. All her cooking was done on a large number nine cast iron stove without the added timers, thermometers and other gadgets used on modern electric stoves. With no electricity there were no refrigerators, hence no meats, pork, chicken, or perishable foods. Yet she was able to place on the table, every single day, a delicious, cooked meal for dinner. When she wanted to bake something unfamiliar to her, she would get one of us to read the recipe. She only needed to hear it once. Months later she would use that same recipe without our help. How often have I dreamed about the aromas from her kitchen when I came through her kitchen door from school!

On Sunday morning, Mom always prepared and cooked the Sunday dinner, but in the evening, she attended the church service. She used to strut very proudly in later years when the minister was away and I did the service. She embedded in me the idea that I should always make sure I was clean and dressed in my best clothes when I went to church. She used to say "you are going to the most important house you will ever enter. You go to be in communion with God, so dress and act your best."

Even today I can't go to church unless I'm dressed my best with shirt and tie. I attended once in my jeans and for the whole service I was so very uncomfortable that I could almost feel Mom's disapproval, even though I was far away from home. It doesn't bother me what others wear in church, but I have so much respect for my mother's teaching that I always find myself uncomfortable and uneasy if I don't respect them.

My mother was as frank and honest as she encouraged us to be. She spoke her mind the way she found things. I believe she was the only woman in Rose Blanche in 1948 that wasn't in favour of confederation with Canada, and she wasn't hesitant in explaining to her friends her reasons why. Many of the concerns she raised about joining Canada have since proven to be challenges for Newfoundland and Labrador in confederation. If she were around now, I'm sure she would seem justified in saying I told you so.

Even though Mom had no formal education herself, she recognized its value and did everything in her power to make sure her children, all of us, had as much as we were capable of getting in Rose Blanche. Money was very scarce in those days, but Mom always made sure she had enough saved to take care of all the necessities we needed for school. She even went to work at the fish plant one year, to make enough money to send me to the teacher's training summer school in St. John's.

Mom always insisted that I had to stay in school even when most boys my age left school and I wanted to leave too. Mom was determined that I would get my grade eleven (school graduation at the time) partly because the minister, Reverend Parish, took a personal interest in me and convinced Mom that I should remain in school. Years later she framed my degrees and army commission, and few people who ever came to our house left before she showed them off. She was almost as proud of my success as I was of having her for my mother.

A Quiet Man

Dad was born in Rose Blanche. When he was ten years old, he left school to go fishing with his father. He thus had very little education. He used to jokingly say he read, in his reading book, that Tom threw a stick in the water for his dog, but he left school before he found out if the dog fetched it or not.

When Dad was a young man, he and his friend joined an American schooner. The schooner had arrived in Rose Blanche loaded with salt cod, but the owners of the boat ran into financial troubles and the boat and its contents were seized. It laid tied to a wharf in Rose Blanche all winter. During this time, several of the crew members left and went home. When the owner's financial difficulties were settled in the spring, the schooner needed two men to supplement the crew. Dad and his friend went to the United States on the boat, and they stayed several years, fishing on American trawlers. Dad eventually returned home, got married, and spent the best part of his remaining years as a fisherman or plant worker in Rose Blanche.

My dad was a simple man, but he gave me several pieces of advice that I have always treasured and have tried very hard to adhere to. He said "George, never argue with a fool because if someone is listening, he won't know who the fool is." This advice has prevented me from entering many senseless arguments concerning religion and especially politics. He also said, "always remember that God gave you two ears and only one mouth." I have found this piece of advice difficult to practice on more than one occasion and I'm still trying to do that one justice.

My dad had a wonderful sense of humour, and a calm demeanour. I can't remember ever hearing him say an angry word, swear, or ever lose his temper. His approach to troubles was a life-long lesson for me, even after I moved away.

I came home on vacation one year, and he and I went outside the harbour to try to jig a few codfish. In those days, when you went out on the water you carried a shot gun. Any time you might get a shot at a duck or some other of the edible birds that continually flew along the coastline. Dad was reputed to be an excellent shooter so when I saw two ducks heading towards us, I waited for Dad to take the shot. He missed. The birds kept on flying. I laughed out loud at him for missing the birds. Without a smile he turned to me and said, "laugh all you want to, my son, but you are witnessing a miracle because there flies two dead birds."

Another time, I had to replace a rotted board in the eaves. The old hammer's head was worn so round that I was missing every second hit at the nail. I lost my patience and flung the hammer away. It bounded down the bank. Dad, who had been holding the ladder, quietly went down over the bank, retrieved the hammer and when he passed it to me, he said "George, don't fling it so far the next time. I find it too difficult to climb up and down that steep bank." That was his quiet way of reprimanding me, and it was effective—I was ashamed of myself for losing my control. Later, even when I missed the nail and gave my thumb quite a smack, I kept my cool and didn't say a word.

I learned a number of adages from my dad referring to the weather. The one I liked best was regarding the way the wind blew. He said:

> When the wind blows from the North
> Fishermen should not go forth
> When the wind is from the South
> It blows the bait from the fish's mouth
> When the wind is from the West
> That's the wind men love the best
> But when the wind is from the East
> It's fit for neither Man nor Beast

Since there were no ground hogs in Newfoundland, February second was called by its English name of Candlemas Day. The jingle I remember is at odds with what I hear on the mainland. In my memory it went as follows:

> If Candlemas Day is fair and fine
> The worst of Winter is left behind
> If Candlemas Day is dark and glum
> The worst of winter is yet to come.

We also had several well-known predictions based on what was seen in the sky:

> Red sky in the morning, sailors take warning; Red
> sky at night, sailor's delight

A haze around the moon, would portend bad weather to come.

If you could hang a powder horn on a crescent moon, fine weather would follow.

A cloud formation called the mackerel sky (like scales on a mackerel) also indicated fine weather to come.

In his later years, Dad had several serious illnesses but even during those times his outlook and humour didn't change. He loved his pet cat almost as much as he liked his game of crib. And when he lost a game, he blamed it on that darn 'carner' that he had trouble with on his way to the 'finishing hole.'

Roots of Kindness and Generosity

My mother's father, Grandfather Strickland, had carved a family farm out of the wilderness in East Bay, Lapoile, where she was born and raised with her many siblings. The Strickland family can be traced back to the 1700s when they occupied an island near present day Burgeo after leaving England. From the island they moved to Little Bay, Lapoile, then on to North Bay Lapoile, and from there grandfather and his brother John settled in East Bay.

When I first met Grandfather Strickland, he had a long flowing white beard. I had never seen a bearded man in Rose Blanche before, so I thought he was Santa until Mom corrected me. Grandfather was a member of the Methodist religion. At night you could hear him saying his prayers loudly throughout the house. He could be very contrary at times, but at other times he would give you the shirt off his back.

I used to stare in awe at Grandmother Strickland. She was a tall slender woman who always wore a long black dress that reached to the floor. When she moved, she seemed to be gliding along instead of walking. I was not very old when I visited her home in East Bay, but I can still remember her beautiful rose garden and her home made bread covered with her jam and cream. She was a quiet woman, but I remember her being so very kind to me. I loved to occasionally hold onto her hand, and she would look down and give me the most beautiful smile I have ever seen followed by a lingering hug. She was truly a lovely lady and she left me with a precious memory that I still love to recall.

William Rose, my father's father, was born in Rose Blanche in 1866. He died shortly after I was born, so I know little about him. I only know what members of my family said about him, which was always good. His father, my great grandfather, came to live in Rose Blanche by way of Hermitage Bay sometime in the 1830s. He was probably brought to Newfoundland by the Jersey men who had a plantation in Harbour Breton. When fishing grounds around Hermitage Bay got crowded, he moved up the coast to Rose Blanche.

I was fortunate to know Grandmother Rose for many years, and she was the model of a loving grandmother. She was always calm and serene, and had smile permanently etched on her face. She dressed in dark clothes, but wore a white apron. I can still close my eyes and see her rocking back and forth in her rocking chair while knitting.

When I was in grade three and four and while Uncle Bill was away, she was alone. I loved to go and stay with her, and be spoiled. In cold winter nights, she would put a medium sized birch junk of wood in the oven after supper. After it warmed up, she'd wrap it in a towel and place it at the foot of her bed, that was covered by her thick home made quilts. I remember the warmth on my feet as I read to her from my schoolbooks. Then it was off to sleep as I cuddled as close as I could to her. I always felt so safe and secure with Grandmother Rose.

With all of my grandparents such kind and loving people, it is easy to see how my mother learned her strong moral beliefs and firm yet gentle guidance, and my father learned his calm and positive outlook. I hope I have been as good a model for my children and grandchildren.

Honouring Uncle Alonzel Rose

When World War One broke out in 1914, Britain called on all of her dominions for help. Newfoundland was the first to offer an enlistment of five hundred young men, called the blue puttees. Most of the young men who enlisted first came from the capital city area. Later, on many young men from the outport areas on Newfoundland answered the call. There were several reasons why they enlisted. Some went because the felt that the mother country was in danger, and they ought to help to protect her. For loyalty to Britain, they joined the army. Others from the outports saw the war as a chance to get out of the confinement of their small fishing community and see the world. They thought, like many, that the war would be over by Christmas and by the time they finished training Britain and France would have won the war. However, the war dragged on.

In 1916, while my grandfather and my father were down in Lapoile Bay to get a load of wood, my Uncle Alonzel Rose slipped away to Port aux Basques. Alonzel was 15 years old, but big for his age. He lied about his age and enlisted in the army. The Newfoundland regiment had just fought a disastrous battle and with the regiment needing replacements they didn't ask too many questions. Uncle Alonzel was sent overseas, and he had his sixteenth birthday in a trench in France. Grandmother often said she prayed and worried more about him than about the rest of her four children put together.

In Grandmother's front room there was a large photo of him in his uniform. As a boy growing up, I admired that picture and from it I got the idea that someday I too would be wearing that uniform like him. He seemed so poised and proud. I don't know what action he saw. Like most veterans, when he came home, he never talked about his experiences in the war.

During World War Two, Uncle Alonzel was too old to be accepted into the army, so he joined the merchant marine. In 1941 the *SS Grayburn*, the ship on which he served, was torpedoed in the English Channel. I later talked with a Mr. Fudge, who was a shipmate of Uncle Alonzel. Mr Fudge managed to board a lifeboat as the ship went down. From the boat, he saw my Uncle Alonzel trying to cut free a raft on the top deck, but the ship went down very quickly.

When Grandmother Rose got the news of his death, she never recovered and shortly afterwards she passed away. Uncle Alonzel is remembered in the Anglican Church in Rose Blanche by stations of the cross that were purchased in England with money he had deposited there. His name is also on the Halifax Memorial (sometimes called the Sailor's Monument) in Point Pleasant Park, in Halifax, Nova Scotia.

I did eventually enlist. In 1961, I was called back to service, and I was so happy to be placed in the second battalion of the now Royal Newfoundland Regiment. I was an officer instructor in Uncle Alonzel's old battalion. Enrolling in his old regiment was one of the most memorable days of my life.

Uncle Alonzel

Chapter Five

My Early Years

I was quietly ushered onto the world stage on November 23, 1932. The miraculous event occurred on a tiny sliver of land call then Misery Point, in the isolated fishing community of Rose Blanche, on the southwest coast of Newfoundland. I have never been able to get in touch with anyone who witnessed any spectacular or miraculous phenomenon that heralded my coming into this world. I probably should have chosen a more suitable time and a different place to debut my grand entrance onto this planet but, in retrospect, I realize I didn't have much control over the situation.

My birth wasn't as newsworthy as other notable events that overshadowed my arrival. The whole world was in the grips of the great depression and, closer to home, a raging Nor'easter was bathing my birthplace with a large batch of snow. Earlier that year, the Toronto Maple Leafs beat the New York Rangers in three straight to win the Stanley Cup (maybe someday miracles might happen again). Other notable events included the New York Yankees winning the World Series over the Chicago Cubs, and Gene Sarazan won the U.S. Open with a score of 268.

In Newfoundland itself, the United Newfoundland party, led by Frederick Alderdice, had won the June election. They defeated the scandal-riddled Liberal government, led by Sir Richard Squires. However, like most politicians, Alderdice's promise to consult the people before any important decision about the future of Newfoundland was quickly forgotten once he was elected. A proud self-governing dominion was thus handed over to the arrogant English who reduced it to colonial status. Although I am a proud and loyal Canadian, I have always considered myself to be first and foremost a proud Newfoundlander since I was fortunately born when it was an independent country.

Baptism

Although Japan had just occupied Shanghai and President Roosevelt had defeated Herbert Hoover in a landslide victory, a more important event on my young calendar was my upcoming baptism. Being born into a Church of England family, it was assumed that I had entered this life burdened with a multitude of sins committed in the Garden of Eden by Adam and his spouse Eve while playing snakes and apples. To save my poor young immortal soul from eternal damnation, it was imperative that I be baptized as soon as possible so these inherited sins would be washed away.

I shudder, even today, to think what might have happened if I became seriously ill and expired before receiving that sacrament. Why, my poor mortal body would not have been allowed to be buried inside the cemetery! But perhaps just as important, at least to me, was that at this ceremony I would be labelled with a name.

There was no minister in Rose Blanche when I was born. The Reverent from Port aux Basques would periodically visit to administer to the congregation. A week after I was born, he arrived for a short visit. Mom was advised to get me baptized then since he wouldn't be back again for some time. At that time, women would remain in bed for at least ten days after childbirth so the onerous task of taking me to church was passed on to my dad's sister, Aunt Alice.

On very short notice, my aunt was required to procure the baptismal regalia for me, find two males to be my godfathers to sponsor me, and then trudge through knee deep snow, with a week-old baby, all the way to the church, which was quite a fair distance away. She was taxed to her limit. When she passed me to the minister, and he asked her what the baby's name was, Aunt Alice's mind went blank. She couldn't remember.

Mom had a brother named Percy who had drowned, the previous August, while engaged in rum running from the island of St. Pierre. Since I was the first male offspring born into the extended family, I was supposed to be named after him. Aunt Alice knew this, but for the life of her she couldn't recall the unfamiliar name. All she could recall was that I was to be named after an uncle in the family. Since there were Georges on both sides of our family she finally blurted out "George."

I don't find anything wrong or offensive about the name Percy, but many a time when someone calls me George or even Jarge, when I'm home in Rose Blanche, I have a tendency to clasp my hands together, look up and silently whisper "Thank you Aunt Alice."

Early Memories

My mother often told me, in later years, that I was a well-behaved baby and that I gave her little trouble (how that would change!). She said I would lie in bed for hours, playing with my big toe or contemplating my belly button. I naturally contracted the young children's infections but quickly got over them. My remembrance of these early years is very sparse. Searching my memory now, I can vaguely recall being swung on my idolized Uncle Alonzel's arm during one of his many visits back from the United States, where he lived between the World Wars.

At about the age of four, our family moved from Misery Point to a house that Dad had purchased in what we called "The Tunnel," an area in and accessed by a path between rocks. I can clearly recall my first visit to that house, walking up the road clinging to Mom's hand. Mom spent the whole day scrubbing and cleaning the place while I climbed over the rocks that surrounded the house. Later that day, we were invited by the kindly neighbour Mrs. Loder for lunch. She gave me the very soup bowl that I used that day and I kept and treasured it for many years. Also moving into the house was my older brother and two sisters.

Mom at the House in The Tunnel. Photo by Lydia Collier.

I started school when I was six years old. I remember little about the primary grades except that I only spent one day in what was called primer and was sent to grade one. In grade three I remember being laughed at because I drew what I called a horse and coloured it purple. It was the only piece of crayon I had at the time.

The Tunnel. Photo by Cathy Rose.

Isolation

The isolation and lack of amenities in Rose Blanche during the 1930s and 1940s is something I frequently mention when discussing my childhood. It was perhaps like the situation in developing countries you read about today, but even the most remote locations people now have cell phones and other services. We had no running water, no electricity, no medical service, no newspapers, not even telephones.

There were no paved roads or cars. Our roads were paths close to the shore, studded with rocks, narrow, and guarded with rails where there were banks. Since everything came by water, houses, sheds, and stores were built as close as possible to the shore. Traffic was entirely by foot. The only wheeled vehicles in Rose Blanche were the wheelbarrows.

The fishermen might see cars, roads, and other amenities in Nova Scotia, but for the children, the only place we could see these things was at a larger settlement that was three or four hours away by boat. This was a trip many did not enjoy taking. Usually, only in an emergency would this journey be made.

Being so isolated could make life miserable for the people of Rose Blanche, such as me in 1940. Charles Dickens would say "it was the worst of times." I was eight years old, and it was Christmas Eve. But there was no sign of Christmas in our home that year—no decorations, no Christmas tree, and no gifts. My mother had been taken seriously ill about three weeks previously. Dad had taken her away by boat, the only option for treatment, but we didn't know where they were, or when they'd be back. We had no way of contacting each other.

Our ten year old sister was trying her best to look after my younger sister and me. I remember clearly, after supper on Christmas Eve, standing behind the kitchen table with my nose pressed flat against the windowpane. It was a calm night. It had been snowing all day and the large snowflakes were still feathering down. The outdoors was covered with snow as if it was especially prepared for a white Christmas. The scene was really beautiful, but I saw none of that. My eyes were so full of tears that I could hardly see beyond my nose. I was a sad and lonely little boy. How I missed my mom and dad, especially at this particular time.

But then through the tears I thought I saw something move at the far end of the path leading to our door. As I wiped the tears from my eyes, I could hardly believe what I was seeing. Coming slowly up the path with her suitcase was my mother. With screams and shouts the three of us rushed out through the snow in our stocking feet. When Mom saw us coming, she dropped her suitcase, held out her arms and enfolded the three of us. When her arms touched me, a feeling that I have never been able to find the words to describe permeated my whole body.

We dragged Mom and her suitcase into the house that was now filled with love, peace, joy, and everything that can ever be associated with the festive season—even gifts. Dad soon joined us, and Mom opened her suitcase partially filled with gifts for us. But that year, the greatest gift I received was my mom and dad coming back for Christmas.

Just as the lack of amenities and isolation are difficult for younger people to comprehend, so are other aspects of that simpler life. People didn't pay property or other municipal taxes and there was no need for licences or permits for anything even if they were available. There were very few restrictions on behaviour as long as it didn't interfere with your neighbour. Animals were allowed to freely roam the community. Most people had a dog or a cat and many kept a chicken coop in the rear of their homes.

There was never any criminal action that I can remember when I was growing up. Sometimes the magistrate from Port aux Basques would visit to settle some dispute about land or fences. I never ever saw a building on fire in our community. Later in the nineteen forties we had a Newfoundland ranger stationed in Rose Blanche. He worked more as a social worker than an enforcer of the law.

Gardening, Gathering, and Goose

There was little gardening in Rose Blanche, due to the shortage of arable land, but Dad's family still had claim on some land on Caines Island, and Mom used a large parcel of it as a vegetable garden. Near the school, and where the Rose homestead used to be, Mom grew a good crop of potatoes, turnip, cabbage, carrots, and beets there. She obtained her seeds from her sister, Aunt Elizabeth Currie, who had a large garden there and produced her own seeds. There was no fertilizer to be bought in the stores, so Mom used fish remnants from the processing plants, and kelp, which was abundant all along the shoreline. Kelp was and is a much better fertilizer than anyone can buy in a store. I had to lug the kelp, in buckets, up from the shoreline to the garden. The labour was quickly forgotten in the autumn though, when the fresh vegetables graced our dinner table.

Another source of occasional fresh vegetables, of which I am less proud of, were the small fenced-in vegetable patches around several houses in Rose Blanche. It took quite a bit of planning and daring to be able, in the night, to snatch a young turnip or a couple of carrots from these gardens. We thought the taste though far outweighed the effort we exerted to get them and the risks we were taking. You could never buy that taste at the local store.

Late in the summer, I spent a lot of time with my younger sister picking berries. Mom and her friend did a lot of berry picking but it was left to me and my sister to supplement the larder. Mom always had a target as to the number of bottles of jam she needed preserved for spreads for the winter.

We usually went berry picking in the morning, so that the rest of the day was ours to do with what we liked. There were a few places in Rose Blanche where the first berries ripened. These were the cloud berries, called by us the baked apples. One kept secret the few places they knew where these delicious berries grew. Several small areas around the outskirts of Rose Blanche were scrounged by us for them.

A large area behind the settlement was called the Burnt Grounds. A small fire had been set on a small level area in Rose Blanche Brook called Handy Hay Ground. It was meant to burn away the bush to create a place to grow hay needed for a cow that a resident kept. The fire went out of control and burned over a very large area, and this became an ideal place for blue berries to grow. We usually carried a gallon can and could easily pick enough berries to fill it in a relatively short time. We also picked a lesser number of partridge berries and sometimes a few raspberries and currents.

An annual late summer excursion to by boat to a large island off Rose Blanche, called Duck Island, was another opportunity for berry picking. The island had a good crop of marsh berries, similar to cranberries. We made a day of it, with a picnic lunch. Mom brought dried fish and potatoes. After picking berries for hours, the meal, cooked with driftwood, tasted much more appetizing and satisfactory than it did at home. I can still remember the taste of catsup on the boiled potatoes, and the delicious peanut butter sandwiches washed down by the tea brewed over an open fire. It was the picnic part of the trip that made it preferable to staying at home with the boys and doing things we always did, including creating a little bit of mischief on the side.

Early each autumn, a large vessel from Prince Edward Island, loaded with vegetables of various kinds, would travel along the south coast selling produce. I remember Dad buying seventy-pound sacks of potatoes and turnip for one dollar each. Sometimes the boat would have other vegetables to offer, and a lucky person might even end up with a pumpkin.

One year Dad bought a goose that was to be fattened up for the Christmas dinner. He even placed a small barrel of water out back of the house for the goose. He took such good care of it that eventually it used to follow him from the shed to its water like a pet. When it was killed and cooked, we all just stared at it, and no one could eat the pet goose. Mom ended up giving it to our neighbour next door.

Chores

We lived in our old house in The Tunnel for about ten years. Then Dad built a new two-storey house behind it. That house is still there. Moving in with us was a stray cat and Uncle Alonzel's large Newfoundland dog named Whisky. With no running water in our house, it was one of my chores to keep the forty-five gallon water barrel topped up. I had to bring water in two three-gallon buckets with a hoop from a stream that supplied water to most of the community. This was a chore I hated with a passion until I read about Tom Sawyer's fence painting. From that, I learned to con my friends into doing that chore for me.

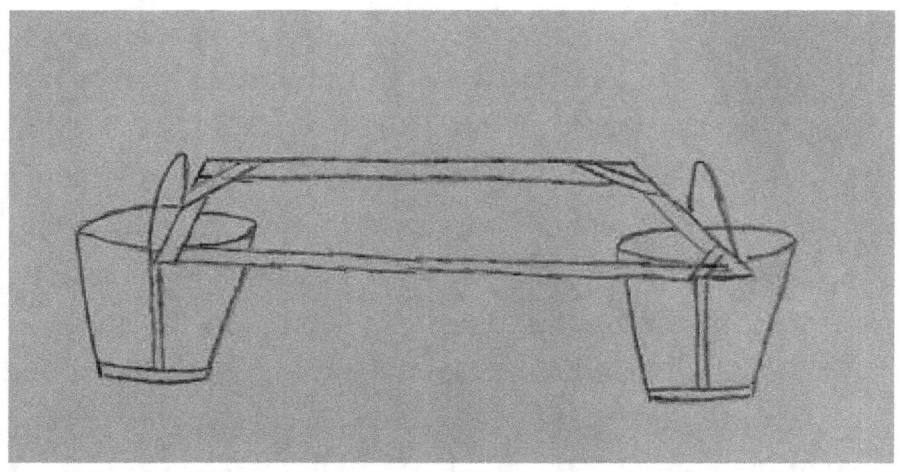

Hoop and buckets for water. Illustration by George Rose.

There were no trees in the vicinity of Rose Blanche, so the people depended on coal as a means of heating their homes and for cooking. Each night, I had to make sure that a supply of kindling was brought in the house and dried to set the coal fire in the morning. And the coal bucket had to be full of coal before we went to bed.

Because of the lack of electricity, and thus no refrigerators, some people, including my family, kept a chicken coop behind their houses to provide fresh eggs and the occasional male chicken for the Sunday dinner table. Another chore I had was to make sure the chickens were fed and that the eggs were collected.

The author feeding chickens. Photo by Lydia Collier.

There were these few chores, school, and sometimes work, but I still had lots of time to do what I pleased. With no TV or other things children have now, we spent most of our time outdoors. To avoid boredom, we had to devise methods of filling in our time with games and activities that appealed to us. We were moving, and doing things, instead of sitting and being entertained by TV shows of videos. I think this developed in each one of us a dependence on our own resources that served us well later in life.

Good for What Ails You

Each year, the government sent to every school a supply of cod liver oil and a chocolate powder called cocoa malt. I remember standing in line with my spoon in one hand and my cup in the other. There was a large copper kettle boiling on top of the pot belly stove in the middle of the classroom. The teacher gave each of us a spoonful of cod liver oil, our daily dose of vitamin D, followed by a cup of the sweet tasting cocoa malt.

Later, the government switched to sending the cod liver oil in small glass bottles—one for each pupil. Unfortunately for me, three years in a row, the bottle slipped through my fingers just as I was passing a large rock in The Tunnel. My sorrow was somewhat appeased when my sisters heartily agreed to share theirs with me. Their reason, I later found out, was that the two bottles shared with three people disappeared quicker.

The Tunnel, with rocks rich in Vitamin D from Cod Liver Oil.

We did not have access to any nearby liquor outlets, and dope was unheard of in the outports in the 1930s and 1940s. Several of the businessmen brewed beer for sale and most of it was consumed when there was a social event called a "time." Occasionally, someone would attempt to make a run-off of moonshine, but they kept it very secretive and only a chosen few would have any chance of obtaining a bottle of that potent drink. A few bottles of illegal liquor were smuggled from St.

Pierre, but Rose Blanche was too far west of the smuggling area to have a big or steady supply.

Hard liquor could be legally obtained from the liquor store in St. John's. A few men would send money by telegraph and the bottles would be delivered express by the coastal boat. One could always see near Christmas time, when the coastal boat came up the coast from Argentia, a couple of men leaving the government wharf with a small brown paper parcel tucked very securely under their arms. Most men knew who had what was called a Christmas bottle and when the time came, they knew which house to go to get a drink.

Drop That Cigarette!

While liquor was scare, to us young boys the bane of our existence was tobacco. Most boys became addicted at an early age and a lot of our time was spent trying to get our daily fix of nicotine. Since we operated under the credit system, money was scarce. One would have to bring, with buckets, a whole barrel of water from the watering hole in order to earn a nickel. Two of us would pool our money and we could get some much older person to buy for us a ten cent package of "Jack of Diamonds" tobacco from the local general store. Otherwise, we would bum or borrow to get a smoke from someone who had tobacco.

One of my most memorable experiences came when I started grade six, and was now in the principal's room in our four-room school. I had just helped a neighbour carry some lumber from the wharf to where he was building a house. He gave me a cigarette for my labour, and I was sitting on a rock really enjoying a good smoke. Suddenly I heard "drop that cigarette, young man."

Hearing such an authoritative demand I did so. I turned I saw my new teacher, the principal. Knowing his reputation, I realized I was in deep trouble. What a way to begin the new school year! The next morning, I walked slowly to school with much trepidation. Just as I suspected, I was lectured for a lengthy period, so strongly that I could hardly hold onto my pencil.

"Who do you think you are," he asked, "sitting there like Winston Churchill with his cigar"?

At the time I was too scared to realize that for the first and only time in my young life I had been compared to such a notable figure, even though it was in such a negative way. This also marked the first time in my life that I shivered without being cold. This event set the stage for the next five years I spent with him as my teacher. He never forgot that incident and I was often reminded of it when periodically he would go on one of his crusades to stamp out smoking among the students.

School and Discipline

My upper grades teacher and I were always at odds, and we both tried to make life more difficult for each other. I don't think it was always my fault, although that might be debatable. Outside of school I was considered a nice little boy, by Rose Blanche standards. After all, I was the little boy who served on the altar each Sunday at the Holy Communion service.

In those days most of the boys left school at grade seven to go to work on the fish plants or fishing with their parents. I was the only boy in my class from grade eight and beyond, who continued with three girls. So being the oldest in the classroom and the only boy, I automatically became the number one suspect whenever anything happened at school. I must admit that most of the time this was not far off the mark.

However, the principal was a real martinet. Most people in our community thought that keeping discipline was the most important prerequisite for a good teacher. He relished this support. He ruled our school with an iron hand and most students, especially the girls, were extremely scared of him. He carried a strap, made from thick rubber, which he wielded at every opportunity. He had a cruel system of strapping. He would hit the palm of each hand, lecture for a minute or two then strap each hand again.

Many years later, he told me that he did this after reading that the first strap deadened the nerves so if it was followed by another immediately it would not sting as much as the previous one. But if he waited one minute the nerves would recover and become more sensitive and the second strap would sting much more than the first.

I was the recipient of many of these strappings for missing a spelling, smoking, suspected of smoking, talking in class, etc. He seemed to have a quota for each day, and I believe he enjoyed administering punishment. Unlike some students, I refused to flinch when he strapped me. I think that irked him to the nth degree.

I admit I always had a bit of a sharp tongue which has sometimes have gotten me into trouble, but I never considered myself as being disrespectful to anyone. I remember one day the teacher drew a caricature of a silly looking person on the black board. He approached my desk and, looking at me with a smirk on his face said, "a good resemblance, eh"? I knew he meant me, but I just couldn't resist saying, "excellent, sir, but you forgot the glasses." Since I didn't wear any and he was the only one in the class that did, his smile vanished. For the next three weeks I had more written homework than I could cope with, but I still think it was worth it. When I couldn't produce the desired results, I was reintroduced to his infamous rubber strap.

But I must also admit that I tried to irritate him, on the sly, as often as possible and he was always on the watch to catch me. More often than not, I managed to get away with it or could get a younger pupil to do it. He'd glare at me when he tried to put his shoes in his gaiters and found them full of knobs of coal, but he couldn't prove it had been me.

We met again, many years later. In the early 1950s, I was called back to duty to Aldershot, Nova Scotia, to help with the army cadets. Being from the regular army, I found myself being my former teacher's commanding officer. How I was tempted! But I kept control of myself and treated him the same as the other cadet officers under my command. After all, I was supposed to be an officer and gentleman by act of parliament, and I managed to practice the latter. Sometimes it was very difficult though.

He and I eventually got to know each other quite well and we came to respect each other to a certain degree. Even later when he became a member of the House of Assembly we often met and talked and laughed about those years at school. We each discovered that we had pegged each other quite accurately during these school years. But even though we were both adults, I found it difficult to completely forget the kind of treatment I received from him during the five years he was my teacher.

That teacher left Rose Blanche, and I had a new teacher for my grade eleven matriculation. I started school that year not burdened with any baggage from previous years. My new teacher encouraged rather than forced us. I found I responded to that kind of teaching with a renewed academic vigour.

My new teacher also encouraged me to develop what little talent I had for writing and a small talent he said I had for painting. But at that time, I was becoming very interested in members of the opposite sex and I didn't feel like I could spare the time and effort to pursue either any farther. It was only after I retired, and with the encouragement of my dear wife, that I took lessons from a very reputable artist named Clarence Osmond and I have been able to spend many enjoyable hours at this pursuit. Now I regret that I didn't pay more attention to the advice of that inspiring and capable teacher.

Reading Time

I always was an avid reader but there wasn't much reading material available in Rose Blanche. I was fortunate in that a minister who had come to Rose Blanche encouraged me to read. He often told me that any person who wanted to become educated should read the classics and, luckily for me, he had large shelves full of them.

He started me off with Charles Dickens' *Kip*. At that time, I was into comics and other light reading so, after reading a few pages, I found Dickens boring. I kept the book for about two weeks and then I gave it to my younger sister to take back. When she knocked on his door and tried to hand the book to him, he told her to take the book back and get George to return it. I could clearly see what that meant.

Each time I returned a book, he would question me about its contents. It was his way of assuring that I had read and understood on some level the books he loaned me. After a while, I appreciated what he was trying to do for me. Under his tutelage, I became familiar with and began to enjoy Shakespeare, H G wells, and other classical writers. In my fourth year at Memorial University, I took a course that covered most of Shakespeare's plays, taught by my favourite professor, George Storey.

In addition to classic literature, the minister gave me his weekly copy of *Time* magazine. Between the American content and news of the Second World War, I found it interesting reading and a change from the classics.

Rose Blanche experienced frequent fog, and at odd times. It would come in over the area so suddenly that two men were needed to man the fog alarm, twenty-four hours each day. To pass away the time, the man in charge did a lot of reading, mostly westerns and other light contemporary works.

Many Saturdays, I would row across the harbour to Caines Island, where the fog alarm was housed, and he would loan me some of his reading material. This became a sort of relief from the heavy classics I was reading. Through the fog alarm crew,

I was introduced to Zane Grey and Louis L'Amour, my two favourite western authors.

Another source of books was the travelling library. Once a year, a box of books came to the school from the library in St. John's. The box contained books suited to the different grades. I quickly devoured the ones suited to my grade, and then those above and below my level.

Chapter Six

Local Characters

There were several local characters in Rose Blanche who amused us young people when we were bored and had nothing interesting to occupy our time. Looking back, as an adult, I have a greater respect and understanding of these people, and an appreciation of how they enriched my childhood, but I'm not proud of everything we boys did at the time. I have not used the real names of the people described here.

The Tinker

Paul, lived with his mother and was an adult when I came to know him. He never finished school and thus had very little formal education, yet he was mechanical wizard and clever with this hands. For example, he was the only person I ever met who could take a pencil in each hand and at the same time write his full name legibly on a sheet of paper.

It was rumoured that he got kicked out of school because he was impertinent to the minister. The minister had been visiting the school, as he sometimes did, and was instructing the several grades in religion. The story goes that the minister said that God was all powerful and that there was nothing that God couldn't do. After a pause he ask if anyone doubted that God could do anything. It is said that Paul raised his hand and said, "Sir, God can't turn a grindstone both ways at the same time." After being suspended Paul never returned to school.

Paul had one of the few gramophones in Rose Blanche back in the 1940s, and a decent collection of Wilf Carter and Hank Snow records. These were our favourite western singers back then. On Sundays, we would crowd into his small house while he played records. When he ran out of gramophone needles, he made his own, and when the winding up spring broke, he made one out of a tobacco tin. It wasn't as strong as the original, but it worked. He seemed to be able to fix anything. I once took my broken radio to him to be fixed. I came back two days later, and he had it working perfectly. He also handed me several pieces that he said were inside but not really needed for the radio to work.

Somehow Paul came into the possession of a one-horsepower gasoline engine. It was old and worn out, but Paul spent hours fiddling with it to make it go. We boys spent a lot of time hanging around to watch him. At first, he had made it fast atop a half barrel, filled with water. After a while he got it working, sort of. He would prime it through the top, spin the flywheel by hand and the little engine would come to life—but only long enough to burn the priming. Later he got a few more putts out of it, and had a crude but effective washing machine.

Paul built his own boat. He cut logs and sawed them into planks and timbers with his hand saw. With few tools, he put together a boat that was a bit narrow, but all-in-all was not a bad effort. Then he decided to install the little engine in his small boat. He made a wooden propeller and a shaft out of a broom handle. The heel of a rubber boot served as a stuffing box. All the time he was working on this, we were watching him, fascinated by what he was doing.

Then came the time to try the engine in its new sitting. But try as he might all he could get it to do was burn the priming for a few putts. We were continually amused by the colourful language Paul used to coax it to go. Someone who knew a bit about gasoline engines, told Paul that his main problem was that the piston was probably worn a bit and as a result the engine had very little compression. It also used to backfire quite a bit too, which indicated that the engine's packing was deeply worn. It was suggested to Paul that if he put about half a cup of warm tar through the priming cup, it would coat the piston and give the little engine the compression it needed to work.

Paul tried the tar. He poured it in, and spun the flywheel. The little engine started but backfired. The warm tar blew out of the engine and, since Paul was bent over the flywheel, he got the full force of it in his face. When he looked up, the only thing that was not black were the whites of his eyes. Paul spent many hours tinkering with the engine, and we spent just as many watching him and enjoying listening to him talking to it, and condemning it for not doing what he so desperately wanted it to do.

Everyone stood amazed the day he started the engine and steamed out of the harbour on his way to Bay La Moine to cut some wood. The boat moved slowly through the water, little faster than a brisk walk. As the day went on, people got worried, and some even suggested we'd better go look for him. We were all relieved when late that afternoon he steamed back into the harbour. He had his boat loaded with wood and it was moving even slower than when he left. But Paul seemed content and was enjoying himself, sitting back in the stern with his feet upon the wood and a cigarette in his mouth. And to top it off he had a smile on his face as large as a dozen tomorrows.

Paul had other interests too, and one was hunting. About nine miles in the country behind Rose Blanche is a flat valley, through which Rose Blanche Brook runs and is called "The Meadows." There is a large flat area between two hills and is a pasture-like place. Part of it is covered with trees. Paul decided to build a hunting cabin there, with little more than a saw, hammer, and an axe. The cabin was small and built of logs. My friend, Ken Pink, and I spent a few nights in Paul's cabin when it was first built.

Since the corner posts of the cabin were vertical, Paul decided that he'd use a large live fir tree for one of his corner posts. Of course, each year the cabin rose on one corner as the fir tree continued to grow. Eventually the corner rose and tilted the cabin so much that no one could use it. It looked comical before it finally collapsed.

Paul lived in a two story house. For a long time, we heard hammering and sawing coming from inside the house and many who passed his house wondered what was going on in there. Then one day we were all surprised to see that his two story house had overnight become a bungalow. No one could figure out how he alone lowered the roof by removing the top story of the house from the inside with the few tools we knew he had. Another example of his ingenuity. He didn't even crack the chimney!

If Paul had been given a chance to attend a vocational school or some other institution, he could have become an accomplished mechanic or carpenter or artisan. If he had, he would have not given us so many hours of entertainment at a time when there was little in Rose Blanche to amuse us young boys. But now I realize his lost opportunity for training far outweighed the benefits we received from it.

Shame

There was one fellow in Rose Blanche that we often took advantage of, and now I feel ashamed of what we did. The young man was a bit slow in developing, what is now called Intellectual Disability, but back in those days we called him retarded.

Billy was much older than my friends and I, yet he acted younger. You could often see him running up and down the road, his trouser legs tucked inside his socks, and whirling a nail on a string or rattling an empty can with a few nails in it. That was his engine, and he was the boat. I mention this because although we should have known better, we tricked Billy quite often.

Most of us boys smoked, and it was a big part of our day trying to get a fix of nicotine to feed our addition. Billy was old enough to smoke and always had a pipe and tobacco on him. When we had exhausted all other ways of getting a smoke and were unsuccessful, we turned to Billy. When we were really desperate for a smoke we would contact Billy, who was always around somewhere, and coax him to play a game of Cowboys and Indians with us.

Apparently, Billy had at one time seen a movie in which there were cowboys and Indians. He was to be the hero, and like in the movie, he had to be captured by the "Indians" and tied to a post in the centre of the fish stage. As soon as we had him securely tied to the post, we would take out his tobacco and take enough for a couple of cigarettes. Billy fell for this ruse every time.

His language became more picturesque when he realized what we were doing. We'd leave him tied for a while and then one of us would return and free him. In no time at all he would settle down. Then a few days later, when he had forgotten it, we would do the same thing again.

Billy eventually moved from Rose Blanche to the mainland. Many years later, I met Billy at a Come Home. I should have apologized, but he had no recollection of how we treated him, and he didn't even recognize me.

The Witness

Another person whom I grew, much later, to respect greatly was John, the Jehovah's Witness. He was, as far as I know, the only person in Rose Blanche who was not a Church of England believer. Every Sunday afternoon, rain or shine, he would come knocking on doors. He carried two black cases, one in each hand. In one were his books, especially the *Watchtower*, while in the other he had a phonograph with a few recordings that supported the religious arguments he would use.

Some people would let him into their homes with the idea they could debate religion with him. But John had the knack of leading the people to talk about the narrow interpretation of biblical subjects he had studied and was very well versed in. He was also very adept in presenting his arguments and could easily debase any rejoinder from his adversaries. When the people saw that they were out-debated things might turn very personal with all kinds of insults hurled at John. "What would your poor old mother say if she knew what you were doing?" Eventually, they would become so angry they would order him from their home.

John always maintained a pleasant demeanour. He never retorted to any insult. What amazed me most was that the next Sunday afternoon he would rap on the door of the very house where he had received the most insults the previous Sunday. He plodded on year after year and, as far as I know, he never made a convert, not even in his own family.

Every Sunday would see him moving from house to house. The rest of the week he was one of the most successful fishing captains in Rose Blanche and he never had any trouble obtaining a good crew to fish with him. How he could endure so many insults and rejections over so many years and still persist in doing what he honestly thought was his particular mission seemed to me a strength of character that was seldom displayed. I grew up with a lot of respect for this man, even though I had no time for any of his beliefs.

Supercallocious

Mr. Brown had come to Rose Blanche from England. With his pronounced English accent and a long list of long words, which were made up by him, he tried to impress us poor ignorant and uneducated Rose Blanchers. He would insert one or more of these long words into any conversation he had with anyone.

He did impress some people, enough to always be called Mister, and that encouraged him beyond sensibility. There's a story that one afternoon he visited an older lady's home, and she treated Mr. Brown with tea and cake. When he had finished his tea, she asked him would he like some more. As usual he tried to impress the woman by using two long words from his list.

"No thank you misses" he said. "I am fully surensified. If I have any more, I would be I'd be supercallocious."

My daughter Cindy always invites the Rose clan to her home on important yearly occasions. As soon as we finish eating, she will always, laughingly, turn to me and ask, "Dad, have you had enough?"

As expected of me I say, "Thank you, but I've had plenty, and I am fully surensified and if I eat another bite, I'll be supercallocious." This always promotes a good laugh all around the table. Thank you, Mr. Brown.

Chapter Seven

A Childhood Year

J ust as there is an annual cycle for fishing, there is an annual cycle of holidays and special occasions, many of which mean more to children. This is how I celebrated occasions and enjoyed the seasons in Rose Blanche, in the 1930s and 1940s.

Valentines Day

In the early grades, we gave light-hearted valentines to every member of our class. As we grew older, we drew the usual heart, coloured it red, and added the words "I love you" on it. I can't remember ever giving one of these to a female class member, even though I would have liked to, many times.

Out in the community we had a unique custom. Up until the last day of February, some people would compose a valentine that was really a song. It would be about some humorous or embarrassing incident that occurred to some person during the past year. The author never put his or her name on the composition. Instead, it was taken, after dark, and tied to the doorknob. After several loud raps the culprit would disappear.

Several of these songs became local folklore, because everyone knew the person in the song and when men were drinking these were often requested. The song invariably received a good laugh at that person's expense.

Lent

Lent was a solemn time in Rose Blanche. Everyone had to give up something for Lent. This was also sometimes called "contrary times," especially for those who were brave enough to try to give up smoking. Sugar in your tea or sweets (candy) were the most common and successful fast. The fasts lasted until Good Friday. There were no dances, card games, weddings, or times (parties) allowed for the forty days of Lent. At home, we were never allowed to play cards during Lent.

On Good Friday everyone attended the three hour service which began at noon. It was the only service where one could enter or leave while it was being conducted. The service itself, consisted of seven parts, corresponding to the seven utterances from the cross that made up the service. People would wait until the end of each short part, when a hymn was being sung, to enter or leave. People did not throw any water outdoors on Good Friday until after three o'clock in the afternoon. I often heard my mother say to do so before that time was the same as throwing water in the Saviour's face.

Easter

So long Lent. A week's holidays from school, and weddings where the whole community participated in the reception and dance. The women's association would host one of their annual times with dancing, soup, and tea. Lent was forgotten for another year and the consumption of sweets and tobacco skyrocketed for a few days.

Store bought Easter eggs were rare. Since we, as most people, had chickens, Mom would save eggs, in brine, for Easter morning. Everyone went to church either Easter morning or evening. For some it was the only service they attended for the year. After morning service and lunch, it was the custom for us boys to go into the marsh behind the cemetery and collect what we called "man-a tea" leaves. These were mint leaves that could only be found in that place as far as we knew. When chewed, one got a sharp minty taste, but we never swallowed the saliva from these leaves.

Spring

During the month of May, large flocks of birds, called King Birds, would fly west along the shoreline. We didn't know where they came from or where they were heading but they flew by in flocks numbering in the hundreds. In the mornings and evenings, men in boats used Black Rock, a large rock protruding from the ocean, just offshore from the light house, as their anchor. The boats would line up about a gunshot apart, in a line out to sea from the rock. When a large flock was seen coming, everyone would remain still. As soon as the birds were in shot, the gunners would stand up and fire their guns. The birds usually flew high over the boats and several gunners would probably get a shot off. Sometimes two or three birds, never a large number, would drop down. Since they would have been shot at from several boats, the dead birds would have to be examined to see which side of the bird received the shot, so as to know who it belonged to.

Black Rock.

These birds were much larger than the ordinary duck and only slightly smaller than a goose. They were especially prized. We young boys were often recruited to assist. Our job was to man the oars to keep the boat in line while the older men awaited the birds. This activity ended when, under confederation, Newfoundland became subject to the Migratory Bird Act.

Also during the month of May, the sea trout and salmon would start returning to Rose Blanche Brook in large numbers. In the evening, especially with a rising tide, the mouth of this small river would be crowded with anglers of all ages. Instead of the regular fishing rods, the fishermen used long bamboo poles. Most were adept at casting long lines with baited hooks. Never a salmon but quite often a large sea trout might be hooked.

Later in the evening, the girls would appear. Across the mouth of the river was a suspension bridge which the locals called "Jiggley Bridge." It could be made to sway from side to side and up and down. Most of the young boys would lay down their fishing poles when the girls appeared. Soon you would hear shrieks from them, as the bridge was swayed and bounced up and down by the young boys. Later some of the boys and girls would pair off, while the rest of us, not romantically inclined, continued with what we had come to the river to do in the first place.

My sister Lydia and her husband Mart on the Jiggley Bridge. Photo by Lydia Collier.

Farther up the river, about three miles, was Big Pond and a level area called The Flats. Land in those places had been cleared of trees and bushes to grow hay. At each place was a small cabin, with bunks for sleeping, and another small building to hold the hay. It was quite an adventure to go up the river and spend a night and catch a whole mess of brook trout, of a species which we called sand trout. These, I suspect, were really young salmon parr. The whole river was full of them, and they were very easy to catch.

The minister, who was also our boy scout master, took us each summer up the river to Big Pond. On this trip he taught us how to safely build a fire and cook a meal. I remember the cooked dinner we had up there each year.

Outdoor Games

We had a number of games we played, depending on the time of year. Most would be the games children played in other places but since we were so isolated for so long, many of these games mutated, and at times, almost beyond recognition. Also, back in those days we had an antiquated idea about the differences between the sexes. We looked on girls as being the weaker sex and did not consider them robust enough to play any games the boys did. The games both boys and girls played rotated with the seasons. After playing one game for a couple weeks, we would rotate to another one.

The boy's games outdoors began early in the spring as soon as the snow disappeared. We began with what we called Pitching Buttons. Each boy had his little button bag which contained buttons of different sizes, colours, and shapes. A stick was stuck upright in the mud. Two, three, or four boys would stand about eight feet back from the stick and pitch one button, when it was his turn, at the stick. Each would usually pitch two buttons, one at each turn, but there really was no limit to how many they would agree on to pitch. The boy whose button was nearest to the stick received the chance of collecting all the pitched buttons, shake them and drop the buttons on the ground. All those showing heads were his. Bottoms up went to the second place person and the buttons were shaken in turn until all the buttons were claimed. Then the pitching began again. Some boys were very adept at pitching the buttons and usually had a bulging button bag. My bag was usually as flat as a pancake.

We played what we called Ball but not by any baseball rules I ever heard of. Our game was called hit and run. You were only given one pitch to hit and if you hit it or not you dropped the bat and headed for first base as fast as you could run. First base was a large rock on the side of the road. There was not a level field in Rose Blanche to play on. A similar rock, diagonally from the first, was second base. There was no third base. The two oldest boys took did the pitching and catching. They had no intention of letting you hit the sponge ball with the picket we used for a bat. The pitcher would underhandedly toss the ball high over the head of us smaller boys and we would usually swing at air. The catcher would be sure to catch the ball. You would have to drop the bat and start your run to first base. The catcher then took great delight in throwing the ball, with as much force as he was able, to hit the batter in the posterior or back.

The only way to get to first base, I found, was to drop the bat as soon as the ball left the pitcher's hand. If you could manage to get to first base safely, it was easy to get to second base and then home, since the catcher was intent on trying to hit the batter following you. If he happened to miss his throw at the batter the sponge ball would bounce high and by the time the out fielders ran it down, you could get home from second base. If you made it home, you could come to bat again. If you were struck out, you had to sit until everybody else was out and the rotation would start again. I can still remember some of the hits on my rear end and how gingerly I sat on the edge of my chair after a game of ball. Why did we play such a game? When the two oldest boys said you were going to play a game of ball, you either played or faced the consequences.

Another game we played was Follow the Leader. One person, whom we knew to be very athletic, would be chosen as leader. He would perform athletic and endurance feats and the rest of us would try to do as well or better than he did. It would involve lifting objects, push-ups, chin-ups, running, and anything else he was good at. One exercise that was usually done was to jump up from beneath the fish flake, grasp the small sticks that were the base of the flake, and go hand over hand, about two or three feet off the ground, as far as you could go. This exercise helped me a lot when I had to go hand over hand on the monkey bars above muddy hole on the obstacle course at the army training camp in Camp Borden.

A game we played, I believe to be peculiar to Rose Blanche, was called Cutter. I think we were trying to emulate some of the adults who were very adept at smuggling goods from the mainland as well as liquor and cigarettes from St. Pierre, off the south coast of the island. One boy would be designated as the government patrol boat, locally called the cutter. The rest of us boys would secrete a remarkable rock or some distinguished token, agreed upon at the beginning, somewhere on our person. At different places along the town roads were home ports where you would be safe from the cutter. In between those, the cutter would hide and as you proceeded, usually running, from one port to another he would try to catch you. If he could touch you, he would be able to search your person and if he found the hidden token then you would become the new cutter. The chase would continue until it became too dark to play the game.

Although we like playing games, we spent more time with our fishing poles, catching anything that would grab our baited hooks. At night we usually gathered on wharves and spent time catching conners (perch), scopins and flat fish. Sometimes we might be lucky enough to catch a tom cod. Our favourite places were on Art Dolomount's liver house wharf and Uncle Jack Wells's rock, just a small distance down from his house, on Misery Point.

The girls didn't play the robust games like the boys did. They had a wide variety of games as well as playing house and with their dolls when they were very young. Boys usually avoided their games because if you ever took part in them, you were called a sissy. But we often stood back and watched what they were doing.

For Hopscotch, the girls would draw their pattern on the road. That was almost the only level place to play, apart from a small empty playground in front of the school. The girls would use a rock to pitch in the appropriate square and then hop the pattern to pick it up. Passersby would move to the edge of the road so as not to interfere with the girls' game. The girls also did a lot of rope skipping. This was often done solo or with two girls, one on each end, swinging the rope while the other girls would take turns jumping the rope.

Early in the spring, while the boys were Pitching Buttons the girls would be playing marbles. Their favourite game was for one girl to toss five marbles in the air and catch them all in one hand. If successful, she put four marbles on the ground and, tossing a marble in the air, she would in turn pick up one, later two and three and then four, and each time catch the tossed marble as it descended. Any miss in the process, and the player would lose their turn and the next player would begin. When her turn came again, she would have to start from the beginning.

Later, when it got a bit warmer outdoors, the girls would play a game similar to musical chairs but without chairs. They would form a ring, holding hands, with one girl outside the circle. She would slowly walk around the ring and then suddenly touch one of the girls. Both of them would then race around the ring in opposite directions to try to be the first to reach the space that had to be left open by the touched girl. The first to reach it took possession of that space and the other girl now walked around the ring to begin the process again.

The girls also played Farmer in the Dell. Again, the girls would form a ring, but this time one girl would be in the middle of the circle. She would be the farmer. As the girls, forming the ring, moved slowly around the farmer would choose another of the girls to be the farmer's wife. She would leave the ring and go inside the circle to stand with the farmer. The wife chooses a nurse, and the game continues with the choice of dog and a bone. Then the process of leaving the circle in reverse order until the bone stood alone. While this was going on the girls forming the ring would be singing not only "The Farmer in the Dell" but verses telling who was choosing whom and who was leaving the circle. Eventually the bone would then become the farmer and the game would start over again.

The girls would also play Patty Cake to a tune they would sing while playing. Two girls stood in front of each other and clapped their hands together and also touching themselves. Some girls were so proficient at this that one could hardly keep track of how they were moving their hands. This game should have told us there was more to girls than sissy ways and beautiful looks.

"King William was King George's Son" was a tune used by the girls who again formed a ring around a girl in the middle. This song required the girl to name a boy she was interested in to complete the song. If we were not playing a game, we boys would often watch the girls to hear which boy she would name. Since the girl in the middle was usually the most popular girl in the school, we kind of kept our fingers crossed, hoping to be the one. Once we heard whom she had named we could cover up our disappointment by teasing that boy for at least the rest of the day.

We also played Hide and Seek, and there were plenty of places to hide in Rose Blanche. Hide and Seek, and Titeley, were the only games which boys and girls sometimes played together, though not very often. Titeley, Rose Blanche style, had two bases set up about twelve feet apart. The home base was made of two large rocks about a foot from each other. A small stick was placed to span the space between the two rocks. The other base was a rock placed on the ground. The person at bat would use a much larger stick to flick that smaller stick as far as he or she could. If a member of the opposite team caught the small stick that side would then be out. If flicked away from the defenders and fell to the ground the batter would run from base to base and each round trip would count five points. The opposing side would rush to pick up the stick and run to catch the runner off base. If the runner was caught off home base, they were out, and the other team would now flick the stick. It would be agreed upon, before the game started, how many points were needed to constitute a win.

These games were played while we were very young boys. When we grew older our interests changed from games to the fair maidens in our midst and different games entirely took up most of our time.

Summer

As it got warmer, fresh breezes kept the summer days bearable. Being outside in the cool evening breezes, scented with the salty tang of the sea, is something I have dearly missed in other places I have lived.

During the summer, we boys spent a lot of time in boats. We made many trips to the outlying islands where we could pick periwinkles and boil them on the beach. There were several small beaches, rocky and not much sand, on that part of the coast. Sometimes, especially in August, when the water warmed a bit, lobsters would migrate closer in to shore to the shallower waters and then we could poach a few. All one needed was an iron hoop from a barrel, a piece of netting, and a cod's head to entice the lobster from its hole, under a large rock. How delicious was a lobster, boiled in sea water, and eaten, in the fresh air, on the beach.

We were in the water as well as on the water as soon as school closed in June. There were several swimming places. but our favourite was Frenchman's Pond. It was rumoured that a Frenchman had drowned in the pond, hence its name. Because of the history, there was one section we never swam in.

Everyone who came to the swimming hole had to undress and get in the water. We always swam in the nude. The more experienced would swim and dive from a rock shelf while the less experienced stayed in the shallow water.

At about the age of six, I still couldn't swim. I never admitted it, but I was scared of the water, especially if I got a few drops up my nose. One evening my older brother offered to take me on his back and I foolishly climbed on. He swam out to where the water was over my head and then he dived. I let go of him and immediately sank below the surface. Somehow, I floundered my way to shore. Coughing and blowing the water out of my mouth and nose, I finally settled down and came to the realization that I hadn't drowned. In this strange and unorthodox way, I overcame my fear of the water and very soon afterwards I was swimming like all the rest. I later realized my brother was very close and keeping an eye on me while I was floundering ashore.

We swam in Frenchman's Pond for the whole month of July but when August came, for fear of what the older folks called the fever, we moved to Rose Blanche Brook. There we swam at a place called Handy Hayground, in the cool moving river water.

Very seldom did we ever swim in the salt water, despite the islands that protected the harbour and the many inlets. Besides being cold, even in the summer, the water was contaminated with waste from the houses and boats.

Halloween and Ghosts

We never did "trick or treat." About all we did for Halloween was draw a few jack-o-lanterns, witches riding a broom, and a few black cats and bats, and paste them on the school windows. We didn't have local access to any pumpkins, and I don't think any were ever grown locally. However, we had lots of ghost stories that were told and retold, especially at night when they seemed to be the scariest.

One of the most often told stories was the rumour of a little boy who periodically makes a sudden appearance in the rocking chair in the kitchen of the light house. He sits there for several minutes and then slowly fades from sight. Others say a young man is seen on his way down the path to the fishing stage where he committed suicide. However, I have never been able to find anyone who says that they actually saw either of these apparitions.

We believed that after dark was when ghosts became most active and we seldom went near certain places in Rose Blanche, alone, late at night. I had one experience though that stayed with me for quite some time even after it was explained away.

On Christmas Eve in 1936, the schooner *Monica Hartly* ran ashore in Salmon Net Gut, underneath the light house. The next morning, the crew members' bodies were found floating nearby and were brought and laid out in one of the stores owned by Newman brothers in the settlement. The store was close to the road. It was rumoured among us boys that strange sounds were heard, at night, coming from that store. We kept our distance from that area after dark.

One night I was out late and alone, and walking up the road past the store. As I neared the store, I was whistling to keep up my courage up when I heard a sudden thunderous "bong" coming from the store. I don't know how high I jumped but I do know that if I were timed, I'm sure I qualified for the Olympic hundred yard dash on my way home.

Much later, it was explained to me that there were several empty forty-five gallon gasoline drums on the wharf near the store. In the daytime, under the warm sun, the air inside the drums expanded and the covers on the drums were pushed up. At night, the air inside the drums cooled and contracted, and the cover returned to its former shape. In doing so, the metal flexing emitted a loud bong sound. Though convinced by this explanation, I always found myself wary and whistling as loud as I could, and increased my step, whenever I passed that store at night.

I took great pleasure in telling of my experience, without the logical explanation, to my buddies, and at the same time never once admitting that I was scared. After all, I had a certain reputation to uphold and here was a golden opportunity to enhance it. I noticed that for many nights after, they too avoided being near that store after dark.

Another place we stayed away from was the Buffet house on Misery Point. In January 1925, in a terrible four-day winter storm, Captain Charles Buffett, his three brothers and another crew member never made it back to port. The grieving family left Rose Blanche. The house, in a white picketed yard, had its windows and door boarded up and remained empty all my growing up years. Whenever I passed that house at night, I walked very gingerly and had my whistle going full blast, even though I had never heard any rumours about the house that should have scared me. Much later the house was torn down, and another was built in its place.

Guy Fawkes

A very important event, much more than Halloween, was bonfire night, on November fifth—Guy Fawkes Night. This is a celebratory event from England which was exported to many of the colonies, but has largely died out. It is still celebrated in Newfoundland and Labrador, even by those who don't know the history.

The celebration dates way back to 1603, when James the sixth of Scotland became James the first of England, succeeding Queen Elizabeth the first, his Protestant cousin. At that time, England had deep divisions between the Protestants and Roman Catholics. Since James' mother, Mary Queen of Scots, was a Roman Catholic, the adherents to this faith expected favouritism under his rule. But James favoured neither faction. There upon the Roman Catholics hatched a plot to get rid of James and the Protestant parliament at the same time.

Barrels of gunpowder were smuggled into the cellar of the parliament buildings and one of the conspirator with extensive military experience, Guy Fawkes, was engaged to guard the gunpowder overnight and set it off when the King opened parliament.

However, one of the plotters had a very close friend in parliament and didn't want to see him dead. He sent him a note warning him not to go to parliament the next morning because something terrible was going to happen. The friend, expecting a plot, took the note to the authorities who immediately began a search of the parliament buildings. They discovered the gunpowder and Guy Fawkes, sitting with it and equipped to set the powder off.

Fawkes and other conspirators were arrested, tried, and later hanged and the plot was thwarted. When the news broke out about the plot and how it was prevented, the people were overjoyed that their sovereign and their parliament had been spared. To show their relief, fires were lit throughout England the next day to celebrate. Ever since then, the event has been celebrated by having bonfires and sometimes setting off firecrackers or fireworks.

In Rose Blanche, we boys considered bonfire night one of the most important events of the year. We started to prepare for it as early as September. On Saturdays, we spent time, when the weather was suitable, in the woods, up Rose Blanche Brook, cutting off tree branches which we called boughs. At night we roamed the roads and anything that was left outdoors, and could burn, was taken and stored with the boughs in a hidden place. We carried off boxes, barrels, and once a large group of us carried off an old punt. However, we never touched anything connected with the fishermen even though, at times, it was tempting.

On bonfire day, for the only time in the year, school was dismissed early so we could have time to lug the combustibles up on the hill to the bonfire site. Usually there were two or three fires up on some hills far away from any building. A straw man, dressed in jeans and shirt, with a bottle of black powder placed inside, sat in the middle of the pile which was lit as soon as it became dark. After the fire enveloped him, the powder would explode with a bang accomplished by a loud cheer from everyone at the fire. Some boys made torches from old rubber boots and rags and dipped in tar. Lit on fire, they were carried from one bonfire to the other. It would be late before the fires completely died down. We arrived home late, tired, covered with soot, and smelling of smoke from the fire.

Birthdays

Each birthday was important, but the celebration was modest by today's standards. Mom made sure we had something special at supper time. Since our birthdays occurred fairly close together, one cake usually did for two birthdays. We didn't give or receive presents.

There was one custom that was observed, and I don't know why or what it meant. On your birthday, members of the family would try to grease your nose with butter. I remember spending most of the day trying to evade my older brother, Walter, who tried every trick in the book to rub the butter on my nose. When I got tired of keeping away from him, I let him have his way. I still don't know who was most relieved when the deed was done.

Christmas

After Bonfire night, the next important day was Christmas Day. There was no electricity in Rose Blanche at that time, so very few people bothered with Christmas trees or lights. Those few trimmed trees that appeared were decorated with balls and tinsel, like the one usually in the church. There weren't many trees near the settlement except for some up in the valley through which Rose Blanche Brook flowed. To get a good Christmas tree would take two weekends. The first Saturday we cut a scrawny but straight tree. The next Saturday we went and cut branches, bored holes in trunk of the previously cut tree, and stuck in the cut branches to fill in and make the tree look half decent.

Before school closed for the Christmas holidays, we held a concert which was repeated a second night. It was a good fund raiser to help pay for the tons of coal which our four roomed school burned during the year. We started rehearsing in November. For the last period of the school day, we would assemble in one room and practice our roles.

My first starring role did not go well. Nine of us, from grade one, had large capital letters attached to our chests, forming the word Christmas. Dressed in my brand new mohair sweater with my hair slicked back, I strutted on to the stage with the large letter H stuck on my sweater. When my turn came, I was supposed to recite the following :

> I have a horn
> I blow it loud
> Because I want
> To draw a crowd.

After reciting my lines, I was supposed to put my horn to my mouth and give a big blast. Mom had ordered my toy horn from the Eaton's catalogue long before, but I wasn't allowed to touch it until my debut on stage. I'll never forget my disappointment when I gave my all for a mighty blast from my horn. All I heard was my pent up breath. The reed in the horn had dried up. Much later on I had other starring roles, but my first experience never left me. Thus, I never aspired to become an actor and any talent I had for a thespian career still lies dormant.

We didn't mail letters to Santa. Instead, we made lists of our wishes, mostly from the annual issues of the Eaton's and Simpson's catalogues. When the list was finished, we poked it through the front grate on our old cast iron stove. As the notes were consumed, we hoped that magically the information they contained would be transmitted to Mr. Claus at the North Pole.

The strongest memory of Christmas at home during my school years was the aromas that emanated from our kitchen when Mom prepared the Christmas fruit cake and the numerous cookies she baked. I remember hurrying home from school, running up the path to be hit by the aromas of her baking which, in itself, seemed sufficient to satisfy my hunger. To be blessed by a sweet red cherry, a handful of raisins, a couple of sweet tasting dates, washed down by a glass of Purity syrup was an integral part of my Christmas preparation.

On Christmas Eve, we all hung up our stockings. I always searched for the largest pair I could find. Although we never got what was on our wish list, our stockings were filled with all kinds of goodies. Most were things that were useful, like new mitts, socks or even a new sweater or other garments. But somehow Mom was always able to find a game or toy for each of us. We'd be up before sunrise and would have consumed a good part of the goodies before we went to church. That was a must before we returned home for our special Christmas dinner.

Mummering

It was after Christmas Day that the fun for us children really began. For the next twelve days, excluding Sundays, we would go mummering around the community.

Girls would disguise themselves as boys and boys as girls. With a pair of rubber boots—a couple sizes too large and on the wrong feet—the front and back stuffed with pillows and with a cloth over the face, you were a mummer. You would go to the door, knock with a stick you carried, and ask permission to enter. This request was done on a breath intake with the words "any mummers allowed in." Most knew which houses that would allow mummers in. Others were simply passed over.

Mummers. Photo by Lydia Collier.

If permitted, you went in and sat while the household occupants got a good look at each mummer. We never expected, or got, any cake or anything else. If any mummer or occupant had a harmonica it was played, and we mummers did the best we could at a step dance. After the dance, we'd leave and go to the next house.

Children started early in the evening, as soon as it became dark. Adult mummers usually came around later in the night. Some of their costumes were a bit more elaborate than the children's. Most adult mummers carried their own music—an accordion or harmonica. These mummers came under closer scrutiny with the inhabitants trying to guess who each one was. They sometimes carried a short stick and used it occasionally to discourage people from trying to lift their face covering.

Skating and Sledding

As soon as the ponds froze over, in early winter, shortly after Christmas, those of us who had skates went skating. The first pond that would get ice strong enough to bear up a crowd of skaters was Doctor's Pond. Later, the larger and deeper Frenchman's Pond became the favourite place to skate because it gave us more room to manoeuvre. But the skating season was short. Sometimes there was too much snow to keep the ice clean enough to skate on. Other times, we'd have mild, rainy periods that weakened the ice so that it was not safe enough to skate on.

The large amounts of snow we got and the many hills around Rose Blanche made ideal conditions for sledding or sliding. No one skied. Our sleds were usually locally made of wood with iron-shodded runners. After a rain followed by a frost, the crust on the snow made it perfect for sliding. If one didn't own a slide, he would use a piece of thick cardboard or linoleum, which often resulted in the slide being finished on the seat of his pants. We often times used the local roads in the community, and the shout of "under below" warned people walking on it to go off on the side of the road or risk being knocked down.

Of course there were often snowball fights. Our favourite targets were the girls. We boys threw hard at each other but rather softly at the girls. In a kind of reverse way, it was the custom to throw snowballs at the girl you were interested in, hoping I guess, that she would at least take notice of you.

Pan Jumping

Another winter activity for boys would be jumping from one pan of ice to the other. The harbour would sometimes freeze over, but the undertow would break up the ice close to the shoreline into small pans. The water would be shallow there. We'd run towards shore from the solid ice, stepping quickly on the pans that were too small to hold up our weight if we stood still. If you moved quickly and were agile enough, you could run the course with little difficultly. But if you happened to slip on a pan, which happened often, you could end up in the shallow water up to and above your rubbers. The water was too shallow to be dangerous.

Mom always forbade me to jump on the ice, but I could hardly hang back when the rest of the boys were boasting of their ability in this sport. When I slipped and filled my rubbers, as happened more than once, I was too scared to go home. Instead, I usually went to Grandmother Rose's. She'd hang my wet, woollen socks on the oven door to dry, set me in front of the warm stove to warm my toes and give me something hot warm to drink. She would hug me and say, "are you comfortable now?" Lucky for me, Mom never found out about this arrangement that I used more than once. That's what it really meant to have a kind and loving grandmother like I did.

One of the most memorable times I remember pan jumping was on October fifteenth in 1942. News of the sinking of the *SS Caribou*, the night before by a German U-boat, reached Rose Blanche that morning and the teacher sent me to Diamond

Cove to spread the news. The *SS Caribou* was the ferry between Port aux Basques and North Sydney, Nova Scotia. Of the 46 crew members and 191 civilian and military passengers, 137 people died. There were several people from Diamond Cove among the dead.

After I'd spread the news, I joined several boys in pan jumping. This was one time that I slipped. I didn't go to Grandmother Rose that time, and I had very wet feet for the rest of the day. I was too scared to tell Mom that I had deliberately disobeyed her.

We also rode sheets of ice. After a prolonged period of really cold weather, the inner harbour, Lennies Harbour, would freeze over. Since fishing was done in the winter and their boats were frozen in the ice, the fishermen would have to break up the ice to go to the fishing grounds. As soon as the wind blew offshore and out the harbour, the men would cut a hole in the ice, tie a bottle filled with black powder to a pole and push it beneath the ice. The resulting explosion would crack the ice. The fishermen would prise off large ice sheets with long poles. As the sheets drifted out the harbour, we boys would get a paddle and ride an ice sheet, drifting out as far as the government wharf. We'd get back just in time to get another large sheet of ice.

Making Do

Our life was very simple by today's standards, and at times very hard. But these hard times tempered our lives. We had enough to eat and wear, and we could get the rudiments of an education if we really wanted to. I honestly believe we got more out of life then because we had no other choice but to put more into it.

We depended and relied on our neighbours and they in turn depended and relied on us. When things needed done in the community, we did it ourselves. If my dad walked down the road and saw a plank loose on a bridge or if the guard rail had a broken nail he would turn around, come home, get his tools, and fix it. So would any other man in the community. Today we would probably report it to the authorities and wait a month or more for action on your report.

We not only made do with what we had but we improvised and very little was wasted. For example, a man bought a pair of rubber boots in the fall for the winter fishery. He used them all winter. When the tops would wear through, he would cut the tops off but still use the shortened boots for everyday wear when he was not fishing. When they got more worn and leaked, he further cut them to make what we called shawboos or piss quicks. These were placed near the door for a quick trip to the outhouse. I've seen that the remaining soles would make good hinges for the chicken coop door. Adapt and make use of what you have would have been a good motto in those days.

With no television, computers and games and very little radio or movies, we children had to find ways of entertaining ourselves. We spent so much time in boats, swimming, running, and playing that there wasn't much obesity among we sun tanned children who had the privilege of growing up in Rose Blanche in those years.

Chapter Eight

Social Life

R ose Blanche had two organizations that most men and women were members of. For the men, there was the *Loyal Orange Association* and for the women there was the *Church of England Women's Association*.

Orange Lodge

The majority of men in Rose Blanche were members of the *Loyal Orange Association*, locally called the *Orange Lodge*. Boys, including me, aspired to join this organization as soon as we reached eighteen years of age. What attracted us young lads was the secrecy of the organization and the regalia they wore, but the biggest attraction was that it marked the end of puberty. We were now old enough to take our place among the men of the community. Besides I wanted to see that mysterious goat that was talked about, that used to make so much racket on their Saturday night meetings. (The term "riding the goat" refers to an initiation ritual in the order.)

On the first Sunday of the year, closest to New Year's Day, the Orangemen "marched out." In full regalia, they attended a special church service which ended with the loudest rendition of "Onward Christian Soldiers" that would be heard in the church for the year. They marched through the community after the service, and if there were a sick member they would all visit him. As a young boy, I was amazed by the two gentlemen who carried real swords and marched near the head of the parade.

Orange Lodge.

The two-storied lodge building was situated on the highest peak of land in Rose Blanche. The top floor, where the secret meetings were ordinarily held, served tea and soup. The lower floor was for dancing. On the Monday night following New Year's Day, the Lodge held the first of two consecutive dances or times.

The Monday dance was limited to members and their spouses. The same two men who marched with the swords patrolled the floor and made sure that only sixteen people danced to the accordion music at a time. The ladies, who served the tables, needed two barrels of water for cleaning up. A couple of young boys, often including me, were given access to the first night's activities as a reward for filling those barrels.

The second night's affair was open to the general public and became so crowded one could hardly get around. Between dances, we were entertained by Phil who, solo, danced what he called the swordfish dance. His gyrations preceded Elvis by a goodly number of years.

Orange Association members helped each other in time of need. This including taking care of their deceased brothers' bodies, since there was no funeral home in Rose Blanche. Shortly after I joined the association, the minister was away when a brother died. I was called on as acting chaplain to read the Orange Association burial service at their meeting. The next night, I had to do the same at the higher up Black Night Lodge. On the third day, I did the funeral service in the church. This prompted one old fellow to say to me later "I must say, George, you certainly pointed him the right way and now I think it's up to him if he gets there."

In later years, I realized I wasn't enthralled with King Billy and the Boyne (referring to King William of Orange and the 1690 Battle of the Boyne), and came to see how anti-papish the organization was. I allowed my membership to lapse. But in my childhood, the Orange Lodge played a prominent role in Rose Blanche, and it is still active today.

Church of England Women's Association

The Church of England Women's Association was mostly concerned with supporting the church. However, during the war years they answered the call to equip service men with warm knitted goods. Almost every married woman, and some young single ladies too, were members.

Church of England Women's Association.

The association, as it was called, had two socials, or dances each year. They used these to raise money to pay for the year's supply of coal and other expenses pertaining to the church. In the 1930s, they held their meetings and socials in the school. In the 1940s, they built their own building. In the school, they used the primary room with its hardwood floor for dancing. Another school room was used for soups on one side and tea and cake on the other. A third room was reserved for bingo. I remember clutching the quarter Mom gave me to attend the social. The admission to the dance was ten cents, a bowl of soup was ten cents and after that I had a whole nickel left over to play a game of bingo.

The door usually opened for dancing around seven, but initially there were only young men, men with romance on their minds, along with young girls, women, and children. One person would prepare the floor for dancing by dropping slivers from a candle over the hardwood floor. This made it easier to shuffle along in the dance. Lots of men could play the accordion and it took little coaxing to get someone to take it and play for a dance. You always identify the player as soon as you heard the tune he played.

The men, instead of going to directly to the dance, would wander in groups from house to house throughout the community. In each group there would be an accordion or harmonica player, and a man skilled in step dancing who would step out a jig. Another would sing a song and still another would recite a recitation or make a toast. Each member of the group had to contribute something. After each performance, a bottle was passed around. Mostly it would be alcohol that had been smuggled from St. Pierre, or rum, and occasionally a bottle of moonshine.

Around eleven, the men having consumed most of their liquor, would stagger to the dance. When they arrived, they took over the dance floor. We enjoyed watching the men, many of them now drunk, dancing and cavorting around. It was amazing how liquor could turn an otherwise quiet and sane man into a performing idiot. In their foolish exuberance, the men would swing the women so hard that their dresses would flare out. We young ones, knowing our place, sat there gawking and giggling at what we saw.

Dancing and Desire

The school also had two times each year: One in the fall and one in the spring. This was to raise money for the winter's coal and other supplies that our four-room school needed. These school times followed the same pattern as the association dances did.

The dances served an important social function. Many young men were reluctant to approach a young woman because of his fear of being rejected and thus embarrassed. He could use dances to find out if he had found favour in her eyes.

During a dance, when the dancers did a movement called "right hands to your partner," the young man would be able to grasp the hands of all the girls in the dance. When he came to the girl he was keen on, he would give her hand a little squeeze. If she squeezed back, he would be encouraged. If her hand felt limp, he wouldn't be so pleased. Similarly, at the end of the traditional dance, he would get a chance to swing all the girls. If she cooperated with him and would continue to swing even after all the others had stopped, he knew right away which way the wind was blowing.

These little nuances, though innocent in themselves, saved embarrassment to both young people. Of course, when watching, we knew who was interested in whom and as we sat there and watched the dancing, we saw quite plainly what was going on. We eagerly waited to see what would happen as the evening continued. In a small community like Rose Blanche, everyone knew everyone else's business through rumours and such.

I must add that the flirting antics of squeezing hands never worked for me when I began dancing. I tried it several times, but the girls I was interested in were not interested in me. Whenever I tried it, I walked home alone.

The morning after a dance, we young boys usually searched around the building to find empty beer bottles. Several merchants made home brew for sale. Men would cast the bottles away behind the building when they had consumed their drink. One merchant paid two cents for each empty beer bottle returned. If we were lucky, we might return enough of them to pool our money and get an older man to buy us a ten cent pack of Jack of Diamonds tobacco with the rolling papers included.

Coastal Boat

Another very important social event in our isolated community was the arrival of the coastal boat. Operated by the Newfoundland government, the boat left Argentia about every two weeks. We could follow her progress up the south coast by the reports given in the Gerald S Doyles nightly news bulletin on the radio. That boat was our contact with the outside world.

When she entered Rose Blanche, either the *SS Baccalieu* or the *SS Burgeo*, crowds would gather at the government wharf. This was the only time in weeks that some people saw each other or got together for a chat. There were no telephones in Rose Blanche at that time. Besides gawking at any passengers on the boat, it was the ideal time to pass along any news and the latest gossip. If you kept a sharp lookout, you could see who received an express parcel from the liquor store in St. John's. Such information might come in handy sometime in the future.

On the boats return trip back from Port aux Basques to Argentia, it would bring goods ordered by the local merchants along with the mail and especially the parcels from Eaton's and Simpson's. One watched the freight, keeping a lookout for fresh things like fruit or a side of beef or pork. These things would disappear from the general stores early the next morning.

I remember I kept a sharp lookout, in the spring, for the long bamboo rods that we used as trout poles. Every boy wanted to be first at the store the next morning to get the longest and straightest one of the lot. And in September, we would be sure not to miss the arrival of the boat. We would be there to assess the physical attributes of the new school marms as they walked down the gang plant of the coastal boat.

Chapter Nine

Becoming a Teacher

A fter I finished my grade eleven, I was faced with a decision of what to do. There was no money for college. The only work in Rose Blanche was fishing. I could not see myself fishing, especially in the winter. I used to get seasick when I was on the ocean in a small or large boat and when I was seasick, I was always too miserable to be able to do anything.

I had to do something to earn money—I knew I couldn't just sit idle at home. The school had no guidance counsellor, so I had no knowledge about any other professions besides teaching, from my years as a student, and the medical profession, from my reading. But I had been discouraged from pursuing a medical career.

When I was about ten years old, I was asked by a group of girls to act as their family doctor when they were playing house. They had a girl, one of their group, covered with a blanket and I was supposed to examine her and suggest a remedy. When I insisted I couldn't examine her unless she removed her clothes, the mother of the house was called.

I soon found out from her lecture that there was no room in the medical profession for a dirty-minded young boy like me.

Any aspiration I might have had for a medical career flew out the window at the same time I was so unceremoniously pushed out the door. One of the girls later told me that, after my rapid dismissal, they were admonished never to ask me to be the family doctor ever again. As I saw it, my licence to practice medicine was revoked long before I even had a chance to begin studying for it.

Many Firsts

To prepare for my first teaching job, I applied for and was accepted to a six-week training course, at what was called summer school, in St. John's. I left Rose Blanche for the very first time on the coastal freighter *Lapoile*. skippered by my uncle George.

When I landed in Port aux Basques, I was awe struck. There on the wharf was a real motor car, the first one I had ever seen. I had seen pictures of them but never a real one. Then began a series of events that were all firsts for me. I had my first ride in a car to my aunt's house for the night. The next morning it was riding again to the train station to go by rail to St. John's. My first train ride. I sat in the coach for twenty-five hours to get to my destination. I left my seat for two short visits to the bathroom at the end of my coach. I feasted on sandwiches from the vendors that plied the train at stops on the way. Having arrived safely in St. John's, I managed to get to my boarding house by taxi.

Early the next morning, I walked up Casey Street towards Prince of Wales Collegiate. When I arrived at Lamarchant Road and saw the school on the other side of the street, I realized I had a big problem. Unused to traffic, and unfamiliar with traffic lights, I had no idea how I was going to get across the street. It seemed to me that just as cars stopped moving one way on the street, the light would change and the cars would move the other way. There seemed to be no stop in the moving traffic. Eventually I walked quite a ways up the street and when I saw no cars moving either way, I ran as fast as I could across the street. A big sigh of relief-my first big hurdle over!

As I approached Prince of Wales, I could see two long lineups. A girl from my class at Rose Blanche saw me coming and called me over. She said that before we could register, we had to have a medical. I later heard passed down the line that there were two doctors: a man and a woman. It was also passed down the line that one had to take one's clothes off. I had never been to a doctor before, let alone stood naked in front of one. I kept praying let it be the man doctor. I kept my fingers crossed and put both hands in my pocket to keep them from shaking. And sure enough, my luck for the day held: I got the woman doctor.

"Drop your pants, young man," she said. With trembling hands, I undid my belt and let my pants slide slowly to the floor. I almost beat them there when she said, "and your shorts too." Then she reached forward and took my genitals in her hand, squeezed them, and said "cough." I could hear my heartbeat over the weaselly little cough I made. When she let go and said "next!" I tell you my shorts and pants came up a whole lot faster than they went down.

For the first week I had trouble due to my unfamiliarity where traffic was involved. I usually kept to the same side of the street and only crossed over when there were no cars in sight. Like other novelties in the city, I soon got used to traffic. Over the six weeks I was there, I must have gained at least fifteen pounds. I ate my regular meals but still found room for the foods and treats I had read about and never had in Rose Blanche. How many hamburgers, hot dogs, banana splits, and milkshakes I consumed that summer, I'll never know. But for the first time, these were available, and I had some money to buy them. And every night I went to a movie, mostly westerns. Movies were another novelty for me and only cost a quarter.

Teacher's College

At school we didn't have much studying. We spent six weeks doing practically the same thing over and over. One hour each day was spent practising singing "O Canada" until we had it down perfect. Most of the rest of the time was spent trying to train us poor ignorant "outporters" how to correctly speak the English language. How many times we repeated "I had to laugh to see the calf go down the path to take a bath." I could never work that sentence into my first year teaching and I didn't lose much sleep over trying.

At the end of six weeks, we all obtained a "C" licence, and we were bona fide teachers. On our last afternoon, instead of class we were instructed to bus down to the Department of Education. There the Superintendent of Education would assign each one of us a school. When my turn came, he said "Rose, Lally Cove." I had never heard of the place and didn't know where it was. Later that afternoon, I went to a museum and found it one a large map of Newfoundland. Lally Cove was a small, isolated community, near the bottom of Fortune Bay on the south coast of the island.

That summer I often thought of the old adage "ignorance is bliss." I can honestly say that for the six weeks I spent in St. John's that summer there were many times when I didn't feel very blessed.

Off to Lally Cove

Due to confederation, Canadian National Railways was running the coastal boats, but they were on strike. As soon as the strike was over, I boarded the coastal boat, on a September Thursday morning, to travel from Rose Blanche to journey to my allotted school at Lally Cove. An hour outside Rose Blanche, I was seasick. I remained sick for the whole trip. I could neither eat nor sleep. By the time the boat entered Lally Cove, early Saturday morning, I was a complete wreck.

I arrived at what I later found to be a picturesque little community around three-thirty in the morning. It was too dark to see anything. Since there was no large wharf for the coastal boat to dock at, the boat stopped in the middle of the harbour. A lifeboat was lowered, and I along with my suitcase and two mail bags were rowed ashore and put on the beach. The lifeboat returned to the ship, and she left.

What was I to do? I was glad to be off the rolling boat and to be on dry land again. I was grateful that my sea sickness quickly left me. But there was no one around. I guessed no one knew I was coming. I sat on my suitcase and had a smoke. I could see no movement of any kind in the whole community. No one was astir. After a little while I decided to walk up the road to see if I might be able to see someone. I hadn't gone far when a large black dog appeared. He started to growl and show his teeth. I retreated to the beach and took up my former position, seated on my suitcase, occasionally smoking, and wondering what I had gotten myself into.

Around seven thirty, I saw two women walking down the road towards me. As they were about to pass, I got ready to approach them. Then I heard one of them say, "Oh, there's the new teacher. I'm not going to board him."

"Me neither," said the other woman.

I let them pass and went back on my perch.

They went a short distance, then turned around and came back. I must have looked a pitiful sight, sitting there on my suitcase on the beach.

"In the name of God," said one lady, "I guess I'll have to take him in."

What a relief! No more welcome words were ever heard by anyone.

My boarding missus, as I soon affectionally called her, must have thought I was a very crude person the way I ravenously devoured the bacon, eggs, and toast she put before me. It was my first food in two days.

As it turned out, I don't think anyone ever had a boarding house that was so welcoming and so warm as the one I was fortunate enough to procure. I quickly became a part of a family of two very wonderful people who looked after me and treated me as if I were their son.

A Sweaty Service

News of my arrival spread fast. As I was finishing my breakfast, there was a knock on the door and a pretty little girl said to the missus, "Ask the teacher if there will be church tomorrow morning."

The community of Lally Cove came under the parish of Belleoram. The minister had a sprawling parish and came to Lally Cove for a service once every four or five months. Since all teachers of the Anglican faith were expected to be lay readers in the church and do the necessary church services that included burials and so on, I understood what was expected of me and answered "Yes."

From *The Book of Common Prayer*, it was quite easy to find the Bible readings and psalms for the Sunday service. My boarding missus said she would pick out the hymns and start them during the service. But the sermon was another matter entirely. I found a book of sermons at the church. I don't think I have never come across a book containing such boring writings. They were in a tome written by some English cleric and each sermon was at least thirty minutes long. Much of what each contained didn't make much sense to me but that was all that I could find, and I felt that I had to use it.

The cassock and white surplice at the church were made for a man at least six feet tall. At that time, I was about five feet eight inches and the cassock trailed behind me like a bridal train. I had to be very careful, whenever I moved, to be sure I pulled it up high enough that I wouldn't step on it and trip.

At eleven o'clock the next morning, the small church was packed. Some came to worship, but many came to get a good look at and to hear the new teacher. When I came out of the vestry, the silence was deafening. I was trembling like a leaf on a tree when I saw the congregation. I thought when I left the house that I was well prepared but when I gazed out over the mass of people my confidence evaporated. Whatever in the world was I doing here?

With a croaking voice, I announced the first hymn. My boarding missus had chosen "Lead us Heavenly Father, Lead us." She led the singing and the whole congregation joined in. Listening to their earnest singing, my confidence began to return, slowly, I was ready to give the service a good try.

I was noted for a loud voice and a tone that seemed to be pleasant to most people. After the hymn, I began the service as laid out in *The Book of Common Prayer*. Everything seemed to fall in place. The congregation was attentive, and the children were all well-behaved. The responses to the prayers and psalms sounded very encouraging to me.

It was a bright sunny day and I had made the mistake of putting my cassock and surplice over my shirt, tie, and jacket. As the service progressed, I began to find it warm and started to sweat. Still, everything seemed to be going along quite well and I was becoming more confident as the service progressed.

And then I ran into my first snag. I knew that any little snafu I made would be magnified in my mind and would be an issue to me even if it was minuscule and not even noticed by the congregation. I was halfway through saying the creed when I realized I should be facing the altar like everyone else. Instead, I was looking straight across the church. Though a minor error, that really started the sweat running.

After the next hymn ended, I walked across to the lectern to begin the boring sermon. I stood there with the congregation looking at me and realized I was supposed to say something before they sat down, and I started preaching. For the life of me I couldn't remember what it was. They waited for me to speak but I was dumb. Now the sweat was pouring. Eventually, the missus, in the front seat, sat down and the others followed. What a relief!

How that sermon started and progressed I don't recall. I remember that I stopped at each period and paused at every comma, but what I was reading didn't seem to make much sense to me. I don't know how it sounded to the congregation. And as I neared the end of the sermon, I realized that there were words that I had to say when the preaching was over. Again, I had forgotten them. I improvised. After the last word of the long and dreary sermon, I turned around and murmured under my breath, not quite loud enough for anyone to understand, "Umph_umph_umph_umph" and then I almost shouted "through Jesus Christ, our Lord, Amen." I didn't think these words would seem out of place.

At this point there was a river of sweat running down my back. It didn't help matters when I tripped over my cassock on the way over to the reading desk. I was close enough to grasp the desk before I fell to the floor.

I announced the closing hymn, and the service was almost over. And so was I. But it wasn't over yet. As the congregation sang, two men took up the collection. They used embroidered bags instead of the collection plates I was used to. And now came another problem I wasn't prepared for. Where would I stand to take the collection from them and what was I going to say to bless the offerings?

I hoped the congregation would still be singing the last hymn when the men brought forth the collection, and no one would hear anything I would say. But the men finished the collection and then went to the back of the church and waited until the hymn was over. Then, in complete silence, they marched up with the offering. I carefully walked out in front of the altar and held out my two hands for the two bags. I turned around, facing the altar, and again murmured " umph" four times under my breath, followed by the loud proclamation, "through Jesus Christ our Lord, Amen."

The blessing and dismissal was uttered while I was still in a trance. It was only when I had returned to the vestry, shut the door, and removed the cassock and surplice that my breathing returned to normal. What a relief! Walking home with the missus, I could hardly believe my ears when she said, "You did a wonderful job, Mr. Rose, and we all enjoyed the service." And to compound it, another woman approached me and asked, "When will we have to be in church for the evening service"?

When I returned to my boarding house, I explained all the mistakes I had made during the service and how bad and awkward they must have seemed.

"We didn't notice any of that," the missus said, "and even if we had, it would have made no difference. We are so glad that we are going to have regular services again each Sunday."

At the seven o'clock evening service I was much better prepared. I had everything marked in *The Book of Common Prayer* that I was using. The missus supplied me with the words to say before and after the sermon and I found in the prayer book a prayer to bless the offerings. Every step in the service was marked out plainly in my prayer book. I made sure I took off my jacket before I put on the cassock, which my missus had hemmed up for me. But there wasn't much I could do about the sermon.

I later contacted the minister. He sent me some short, sensible, sermons. After several services, it was no longer a challenging experience to run the service and I soon looked forward to sharing the service with the community.

Keeping the School Open

The next morning, it was off to school and my first day as a teacher. School was to start at nine thirty. I arrived early, though not as early as the pupils. They were all waiting at the door—all forty-five of them.

After they were assembled, I sorted them out by grade, assigned seats, gave out new textbooks, and obtained their payment for same. I discovered that I had grades kindergarten to grade nine. My teaching aids consisted of a blackboard eraser, half a box of chalk, a wooden protractor, and a yard stick. There was also a large map of Newfoundland on the wall.

And so, I began teaching. My days were busy setting copying tasks for kindergarten, hearing spellings, and correcting answers after explaining and setting questions in the higher grades. They certainly kept me busy and, somehow, I them. I spent a few hours each night correcting work and trying to prepare lessons for the next day.

That first week, I operated in a daze. Nothing I had learned at the short summer school prepared me for what I was facing now. I tried to recall the way I was taught in school, but I couldn't seem to remember much that was of benefit now. I did remember though, that I must maintain discipline. Being so inexperienced, I know now that I became too obsessed with that matter. However, I was not as obsessed as my teachers had been. There was a large leather strap hanging in the classroom. I had too many unpleasant memories of my own school days to have that monstrosity around. It went into the fire the first time the large pot-bellied stove was lit.

The stove, in the middle of the classroom, heated the school. Men took turns lighting the fire in the winter early enough in the morning to have the room warmed up before classes started. The men would cut enough wood in the spring, and store it near the school to dry over the summer. Sometimes on Saturday I sawed up some of that wood with a buck saw.

On Sundays, I had church services at eleven in the morning and seven in the evening, and Sunday school at two in the afternoon for the children. I didn't have much idle time. Another part of the job was filling out various forms for people in the town.

And then the coastal boat came with the mail and in it was my first cheque—my first month's pay for teaching. It had cost me twenty-two forty in passage money to get to Lally Cove. My room and board cost me twenty dollars a month. When I eagerly opened the envelope, I discovered my pay as a C licence teacher was fifty dollars a month. I had just finished my first month teaching, with the other obligations, and I could put seven dollars and sixty cents in my wallet. I never did try to calculate what I was being paid per hour for my work, but I know I was way below the minimum wage. However, I had a job; I would get paid each month, and in Newfoundland, especially at that time, not everyone was as fortunate as I was. But there were many times that year when I would doubt if it was worth it.

In hindsight, I wasn't really teaching that year, just keeping the school open. I have often regretted not being able to apologize to those forty-five beautiful children for what I put them through as I made them sit there like little saints while I rushed about trying to educate them.

The people in Lally Cove were very good to me and that treatment meant a lot. I was always called by all as Mr. Rose, and they showed respect by referring to me as sir. They appreciated my efforts and often stopped to encourage me. They, like people in most outports, including Rose Blanche, lived a subsistence existence and had little to give. Yet often I would come home from school to find a brace of rabbits (two), or a couple of lobsters, which they found out I loved, or a couple of turrs (birds, also called murres), and always with a note saying, "for the teacher."

Extracurricular Activities

There were a couple of large brooks in the area, and on a fine Saturday I would take a dory, row over, and spend a quiet afternoon fishing, my favourite pastime. There usually was a good run of sea trout in these brooks and I was able to keep our three cats well fed, as well as ourselves, with this delicious little fish.

The man of the house was a fisherman, of course, and the largest part of his income was from the lobster fishery. During the winter, I would very often join him in his heated shed. He taught me how to build lobster traps and how to knit the headings that went into them. In the spring, I would arise with him on Saturdays, before dawn, and go out with him in his dory, while he pulled his traps, took out the lobsters and baited the traps again. I was expected to put the wooden pegs in the lobster's claws. Reaching into a box of wriggling lobsters to get one to peg wasn't my favourite pastime, especially after having several attach themselves to and pinch my fingers much harder than a hug.

One of my obligations was to produce a school Christmas concert. Some men came in and constructed a stage at the back of the school room. I was left to devise a program that would include each one of the students. We practised the program after school.

There were short skits I wrote, called dialogues, recitations collected from the community and lots of songs, especially by the girls. The whole class, acting as a chorus, did the opening and closing. The people demanded a second performance and on the second night a dance followed to the music of the accordion. Following the second night, I slept in the next morning, and I welcomed the twelve day Christmas break. I was exhausted.

In June I paid my board for the month, bought my ticket back to Rose Blanche and again put my seven sixty in my purse. I was seventeen years old now, had grown about three inches, added a few pounds and had a year's experience under my belt. I had saved enough money from my meagre wages and, with my two summer pay cheques, would be able to attend summer school for teachers again, this time at Memorial University. For the first time, and for the rest of my life, I was able to pay my own way, without help from anyone.

Diamond Cove

The next year I accepted a position to teach at Diamond Cove. This meant I could stay at home in Rose Blanche and walk the mile to and from school each day. With my B licence and the increase in teacher salary that warranted, I was making one hundred and twenty-five dollars a month, and without travel or boarding expenses. I was beginning to feel like I was getting somewhere, and I was now seriously thinking of making teaching my life's work.

I tried that year, at Diamond Cove, not to make the same mistakes I had made at Lally Cove. I had fewer pupils but the same range of grades. The teaching didn't seem as stressful as it had been the year before. On my second day at school a young man, who later became a close personal friend, came to the school door and asked me if he could come back to school. He had been away from school for about five years and wanted to return. I started him at grade nine. He passed his provincial exams that year and continued school, and went on to become a teacher. I always felt proud that I had played a small part in this young man's change in life and his later success.

St. Michael's and All Angels Church. Photo by Lydia Collier.

That year, the minister, who had encouraged me to read and been my mentor for years, decided to take an extended vacation and spend some months touring the United States. Before he left, he asked me to take over work of the church in the parish. I did two regular services each Sunday as well as baptisms and funerals. I was paid, by the parish, two dollars for each service I performed but nothing for burials and baptisms. I kind of smiled the day I buried an old gentleman whose garden I had raided some years back for a few carrots. He had found out that

I was the one and he threatened me every time I came close to him.

The year in Diamond Cove went so well that I decided that I would go to university to get the proper training to become a real teacher. But money was problem. In those days there were no student loans, and the banks wouldn't loan me money because I had no collateral. I decided to teach another year with my current training, so I could save money and get one year of teacher training at Memorial University.

Cape La Hune

For the next school year, I accepted a teaching position at Cape La Hune on the south coast. It was a wise decision on my part. I fell in love with the wonderful people and children in that community. They all treated me like royalty.

The area had ponds teeming with trout and an area with lots of big game animals. My weekends were filled with outdoor activities that I loved and could only be found in outport Newfoundland at that time.

My students were exceptional. I had three boys and a girl to prepare for provincial exams. On weekends, the three boys were my companions on our hunting and fishing trips, and I was treated as one of them. But on Monday morning I was Mr. Rose, the teacher, and was treated perhaps with more respect than I deserved.

On my way home from school, I would very often find Mr. Pink, an elderly gentleman, at his chopping block. I loved to sit and talk with him ever so long. With a little coaxing, he'd sing for me the fine old English folk songs of which he knew many. I never got tired of his singing.

Another old gentleman, Mr. Jim Baggs, would vie with me to see who could tell the biggest whopper. I was invited to ever so many homes for scoffs (informal meals) and card games, and I always got treated with the lady's prized apricot brandy that had been smuggled from St. Pierre. My cigarettes, also smuggled from St. Pierre, cost me ten cents a pack and I tell you I smoked a lot of them.

It was at Cape La Hune, teaching nine grades that I came up with an idea that lightened my load tremendously. Since the older students had brothers and sisters in the lower grades, I arranged the seats so they sat together. The older students were told to keep an eye on their sibling and see that they did their work and sometimes give them a hand if needed. This cut down on any discipline problems I might have had, and I could be a more pleasant teacher rather than a crappy old disciplinarian.

My idea, when I explained the unusual seat arrangement to the government school inspector who visited the school, must have impressed him. After he returned to St. John's, I received a letter inviting me to attend Memorial University and offering me an indenture of six hundred dollars.

The day I was to leave Cape La Hune, almost every family came to visit me and bid me farewell. They each handed me an envelope that contained a small amount of money and a note, which I still possess and treasure, thanking me for the year's teaching of their children. The people had little in those days, but they gave freely of what they had. To cap a successful year, my four grade nine students successfully passed their provincial examinations with excellent marks in every subject they wrote.

A Kitchen Party Toast

While I was away a lot for teacher training and the teaching position, I returned to Rose Blanche when I could. I enjoyed so much my visits at home, especially around Christmas time. Kitchen parties were in vogue. A group of men would move, eventually settling at one house. There would be music, dancing, singing, and drinking, and everyone had a marvellous time.

When it came to singing, the men requested the local songs—true Newfoundland folk songs, not those imported from other countries. The songs they wanted to hear were invariably about some humorous incident about a known person or a tragic event.

One of the most commonly sung was "Tom Bird's Dog." This song tells the story of what happened early one morning when a man left home to go hunting for birds, encouraged to do so by his wife. On his way to the boat, he was attacked by Tom Bird's large dog. The final verse gets the biggest laugh when the wife laments her deep disappointment that because of the dog's attack the hunting trip was abandoned, and she didn't get "her bird." This song also engendered mention in the Newfoundland Dictionary because of a word peculiar to Rose Blanche. The composer of this song was a local wit named Claude White.

Another favourite song, composed by Max Currie, was called "Burgeo Jail." It was about three young men from Rose Blanche who were under the legal age of twenty-one, but ordered and obtained liquor from the liquor store in St. John's. Someone reported them, they were brought to trial, and sentenced to three weeks in the jail in Burgeo. The song goes on to tell how they were kept very busy all the time doing mostly household tasks. Each was assigned a specific task and laboured at doing it. The final verse told how difficult they found it labouring in a confined space with their handkerchiefs tied over their noses as gas masks, since the air was polluted by the effluence from a three week diet of baked beans.

Sometimes a tragic song was requested, like the song entitled "Danny Goodwin." It told the story of a small fishing boat from English Harbour that was fishing out of Rose Blanche in the winter. During a storm, the boat and its crew failed to return to port. There were many tragic stories sung about such events.

Once I was an adult, I could move with the group, but since I couldn't play music, sing, or step dance, I was required to do something else as my part of the entertainment. And what I did best was to say a toast or recitation. I borrowed one from an east coast man, the famous Mr. English, but added local colour to it to make it more attractive to the audience I was with. The men loved it. The toast, as they called it, was rather long but I always enjoyed the effect this had on the group:

I had just finished my grade eleven and was all packed to go off to college. It was early in September. I heard someone shout that the boat was coming. This meant the arrival of the coastal boat and everybody who was anybody, and that included everybody in Rose Blanche, rushed to the government wharf to see who might coming ashore.

As I joined the crowd and approached the wharf, I saw the new school marm coming down the gang plank. Although she was wearing a long coat on, I could see she was young and had the kind of shape I appreciated. As she swaggered across the wharf, with her two suitcases, I silently promised myself that I would be the first one in Rose Blanche to get a crack—I mean get a date—with this new school marm.

Lucky for me, she was boarded at my uncle Bills. In the next week or so I spent a lot more time than usual at my uncles. Since he was getting along in years and was far too busy for a man his age, it was only natural that I'd give him a hand at some of the work he was doing. And besides, I was leaving soon and wouldn't see him and his wife for a long time.

On Saturday night there was going to be a time, a dance, in the school on Caines Island. At supper I said to Mom, "I wonder if the new school marm would like to go to the dance with me."

Mom said, "why don't you ask her? But remember if she agrees to go, you make sure you mind your manners and don't forget after all she is the new school marm."

After supper I got ready for the dance. I put on my new bib overalls, my new yellow shirt, and my matching purple tie. I borrowed my brother's razor and took care of the two hairs on my chin. I slicked back my hair and then rubbed a bit of Vaseline in it in order to make it stay in place. I went out to the shed and got a few felt tins to put in my pocket. When I jingled them, it would impress the girls because they'd think I had a pocket full of money. But I had a problem with my shoes. They were kind of old, scuffed a bit and worn white around the toes. Someone told me once that if you rub a piece of pork rind over your shoes they would glisten. Sure enough, that did the trick.

When I arrived at Uncle Bill's, the new school marm was sitting in the rocking chair—rocking and stretching her gum like a real pro. But as soon as I sat down, I knew I had a big problem. My aunt had a big old yellow tom cat. He made a direct line for my shoes and started licking them. I wanted to give him a good kick, but I saw my aunt was watching me very closely. No matter how much I shuffled my feet he kept licking until my shoes were back to and perhaps worse than when I started to grease them.

After exchanging a few pleasantries about the weather and such I got up enough courage to ask the school marm if she would like to go to the dance with me.

"Of course, George," she said. "I'll be just a few minutes." She moved rather quickly towards the stairs and came back down in about five minutes.

What a beautiful sight! She had on a bright red dress that hugged her in all the right places. It fitted her so tightly I could, not for the life of me, figure out if she was inside that dress trying to get out or outside that dress trying to get in. She had her hair tied back with a yellow ribbon, matching my shirt, and on her feet, yes, my son, on her feet she wore a brand new pair of black rubber boots with the tops turned down about an inch.

She hooked her arm in mine, and we were soon on our way up the road to the wharf. I borrowed Jakey's punt to row across the harbour to the dance. Imagine that! Me, George Rose, in a boat, with the new school marm and she looking as slick as a stick of Wrigley's chewing gum. Why wouldn't I be real full of myself?

When we arrived at the wharf, on the island, I tied on the boat. She climbed up the stage head, but I didn't look up when she was climbing. I had heard that if you deliberately looked up under a woman's dress when she was climbing you might, at some time in the future, have eye trouble and could even eventually go blind. I didn't look up. Instead, I looked across the water at the old granite light house.

The dance was in full swing at the schoolhouse. It wasn't too long before the new school marm was clicking her new rubbers together and cracking her gum as well as the best of them. We noticed that some young couples were going outside every so often, to cool off, I presumed.

"Georgie," not George now, said the new school marm, "I could do with some fresh air." So, I took her outside. She led me around the dark side of the school and when we stopped, she cuddled up mighty close to me. It was hot inside that schoolhouse, but it could get even hotter outside. I began to think that the new school marm was trying to tell me something, but then I remembered she was the school marm and I had to mind my manners.

We went inside, danced a while longer, had something to eat, danced some more, and then it was time to home. I climbed down aboard the boat and untied her. The school marm took her dead old time climbing down the stage head. She got about halfway down when she stopped and just stood there, and smiled down at me. It was then that I decided to test that old adage about going blind. I decided I was going to risk one eye at least. And, oh boy, that was one risk worth taking. It wasn't too long before I had both of them wide open. She just hung there looking at me and smiling. I asked myself, is the school marm trying to tell me something? But no, she's the new school marm and I must mind my manners.

She finally climbed down and sat in the ass—I mean the stern—of the boat and I started rowing across the harbour. I was doing a good job too, considering the circumstances.

"Georgie" she said, "can I help you row the boat"?

"Yes ma'am," I said. She left her seat and came and sat down by me.

"Georgie," she said "can you row with only one hand?

"Yes ma'am" I said.

"Well, you better put your arm around me," she said, "or I might fall off this seat."

She cuddled up even closer than she did at the back of the school. She even pushed my hand well above her waist. And again, I thought, is the school marm trying to tell me something? And I remembered what Mom said—I must mind my manners.

I kept rowing, but I no was longer was paying close attention to what I was doing. The boat jerked to a stop. We had run ashore on a little island about three-quarters the ways across the harbour. I got out to push the boat off, but before I could do so the school marm jumped out and said "Georgie, there's a nice grassy spot up there. Let's sit up there a while and look at the stars. It's a beautiful night."

My Uncle John Rose was drying some salt cod fish on the island, and as everybody knows, when you're drying salt fish the place will be swarming with blue ass—I mean blue tail—flies. When the school marm sat down by me, her dress accidently was pulled up, so the hem was well above the knee. And along flew a blue ass—I mean a blue tail—fly and pitched on her leg just above her knee. I watched, hypnotized, as it walked up her leg and continued on up under her dress out of sight.

"Georgie," she said while looking at me with those large baby blue eyes, "Wouldn't you wish you were that fly"?

The school marm was surely trying to tell me something, and that this was neither the time nor place for manners.

To cut a long story short, about two weeks later I was in my dorm at college, and received a letter from my sister. Among the news she mentioned was how strict the new school marm was. One young fellow was suspended from school for three days because he was looking at her knees. Another young gaffer was sent home for a week because he was looking at her leg above the knee. And as I turned over to go to sleep, I murmured to myself, "It's a good thing, George my son, that your school days are over."

An Officer and a Scholar

In September of 1954, I enrolled at Memorial University as an educational student. I had enough money saved for one year at the institution, but I was not there long before my thirst for knowledge led me to try to find a way to be able to stay and complete a degree.

I found out there was a program called the Canadian Officers Training Corp (COTC). If I were accepted, I could study at the university from September to the end of April, and from then to mid-September I could train to be an officer in the Canadian Forces. While in the army, I would be paid as a junior officer. If I was frugal enough, I would have enough money to complete a university a degree while receiving superb training I would never be able to get anywhere else.

It was difficult to get into the army program. However, the dean saw my position and he went to bat for me. After a number of tests and interviews, I was one of two accepted as an officer in training in the infantry Corp. On May fourth, 1955, I was off to training at Camp Borden in Ontario.

I knew nothing about the army, but I was placed in a platoon of young officers in training from the military colleges in Ontario and British Columbia. They already had a year's training, and I was fortunate that they took me under their wing and mentored me in the routines of training. After they found out I was not a "Goofy Newfie" (then and still now, I consider "Newfie" derogatory) and could keep up to them in the physical training I was accepted as a member of their team.

I came to love the army. I liked the discipline, the orderliness, and the neatness, but especially the comradery that developed among all members I trained with. We came to realize that we were not only responsible for the lives of the young men we were going to lead but also that our own life was going to depend on the young man next to me. Nowhere but in the army could I ever get the excellent training I was getting while at Borden, and which continued when I joined the elite Second Battalion of the Black Watch.

In my first season in the COTC, I was picked to represent the army in a shooting contest, with two other services, for the Outerbridge trophy. Nelson Bennett and I won the trophy two years in a row, and as a result I received a sharpshooter award.

I continued in the COTC program for the next four years, receiving my commission as a Second Lieutenant in the regular Canadian army from her Majesty the Queen. And, as planned, I used my earning to study, and graduated from Memorial University with my BA Degree. Now I was faced with a dilemma.

My time in the Black Watch convinced me that I could very well have a good life in the regular army but my training at the university also led me to believe that teaching was both honourable and rewarding. A close friend of mine was graduating the same time as I was. He was going to be principal of a new modern high school up in Flowers Cove, on the Great Northern Peninsula of Newfoundland. He kept coaxing me to come along with him as his vice-principal. He finally convinced me that I could delay an army career for a year or two to go to northern Newfoundland and teach with him.

The Love of My Life

I met a lot of people at university, including the beautiful Effie in my fourth year. I was attracted to her, but busy with final year studies and didn't have the funds to contemplate a relationship. After I moved up north, I discovered she was teaching the same community where I was boarding.

Now I was ready to pursue her, but how? The opening I was looking for occurred soon. As before, since I was an Anglican teacher, I was expected to hold church services. I couldn't sing, and when I inquired about someone to lead the hymns for me, he suggested Effie.

Saturday night, I dressed in my finest, knocked on her door, and she invited me in. Contact was made and the rest is history. Every Saturday night I came knocking and I was welcomed by the whole family. I proposed to this amazing person on my birthday, and her yes was one of the most wonderful birthday gifts I ever received. We kept our plans secret until Easter, but I don't think we surprised anyone by our announcement. On June 29, 1961, we were married in the church in Flowers Cove on a day that is forever ingrained in my mind.

My ideas of the future quickly changed course. My new wife, the love of my life, preferred that I continue teaching rather than serve in the army, and my interest in a military career faded, in favour of a what became a successful and fulfilling teaching career. I entered the reserves, ready to answer the recall to service if needed. I later did service for a summer in Aldershot, and spent a year with the Royal Newfoundland Regiment. I never forgot the excellent training I received while serving in the army and I highly recommend it to any young man starting his adult life.

My one year up north living in Flowers Cove turned into ten, and my generous wife gave me four beautiful daughters, Connie, Carol, Cathy, and Cindy. For fifty-four glorious years, I lived with the most wonderful person I have ever been in contact with. The angels took her from me in 2015, on the anniversary of our wedding.

Chapter Ten

Life After Retirement

I have had many hobbies during my ninety years, but the one I probably spent most time on and which I've enjoyed the most has been angling. I started very young with a bamboo rod, fishing for conners on the local wharves in Rose Blanche. Later, I spent many hours fishing in Rose Blanche Brook for the yearly run of saltwater trout.

When I was ten years old, I went camping at a place called Farmers Arm River with an old man named Thomas Anderson. He was an excellent fly fisherman and taught me much about salmon fishing, which I came to love. My best angling occurred when I went to northern Newfoundland. The rivers there were teeming with salmon and hardly anyone fished for them. With my summers free thanks to my teaching career, I had ideal fishing opportunities. I taught myself fly tying and always tied my own flies.

Another hobby I had for a number of years was hunting. I had very many successful hunts for moose and caribou with my very good friend Mr. Pink of Harbour Le Cou and Cape La Hune. Later I hunted on the Great Northern Peninsula with another friend, Ron House, and after he passed away, my brother-in-law

Roland Way. I shot my last moose at age eighty, and gave up hunting and angling when my wife and I left Newfoundland and came to Nova Scotia to spend our remaining days with our extended family.

When I retired in 1988, I knew I had to have a hobby to pass away my idle time. I was already interested in woodworking—in 1979 my daughter Carol had asked me to make a gazebo, to be used in her graduation prom for photographs in. I bought the necessary tools, took a course on how to use them, and produced articles like a deacon's bench, and an eight-sided table for my wife to put her family photos on. I also made bookcases, shelves trays, and repaired and refinished a 150-year-old rocking chair for my wife, which she loved to exhibit.

Then Archbishop Payne appointed me Associate Editor to the *Newfoundland Churchman*. The *Churchman* was founded in 1899 as *The Diocesan Magazine*, became the *Churchman* in 1959, and since 2000 has been called *Anglican Life*. It is still in print, and now has a web site. At the time I worked for it, print circulation in Newfoundland and Labrador was about 45,000 copies. I got so wrapped up in composing editorials and reporting on church matters in western Newfoundland and southern Labrador that I gradually weaned myself away from woodworking. I always loved writing and composing stories, especially bedtime tales for my grandchildren, and now great grandchildren. I spent much time writing and taping stories for them to read and especially to listen to when they went on their many trips.

For a while, my wife and I taught bridge for a fee, fundraising to help pay the debts of a new YMCA. In 2000, for my birthday, my wife bought me art lessons from the reputable art teacher Clarence Osborne. I took lessons from him for three years, and completed several hundred pictures which I framed and gave to my extended family and friends.

My love of writing stories also led to this book. After I finished it, my daughter Carol typed and edited the first edition, and planned for it to be printed and presented to me on my 90th birthday. The book sold well in my hometown, with all proceeds going to needs in the community. My daughter Cindy helped prepare an updated and revised second edition.

I keep busy listening to lectures from prominent professors at leading American universities, mostly on the history of people and events that I missed when I attended university years ago. This was a thoughtful gift from my daughter Connie in Montreal. And here at The Berkeley retirement home I take an active part in trivia contests, crosswords, and other games, and attend church services. I help plan and MC the annual talent show, and Remembrance Day celebrations. And I am still reading, thanks to an extensive library here, thanks to donations from people in the community, including author Donna Alward.

I'm still up at four every morning, and start by making the bed—army training. Next, I perk a coffee which I enjoy with two homemade muffins that Carol supplies. I turn on my TV to get the scores of games played the night before and to get the weather forecast. Then over to CNN and NBC to get the latest news. Then I sort out my pills for the day, take care of eye drops, puffers and so on. I'm grateful to my daughter Cathy, who takes such great care of me and my health. It's so comforting to know

I have such a wonderful daughter nearby to call upon when I need her.

I do a couple of crosswords or sudoku, and then prepare my breakfast. Then it's exercise time. With my walker for balance control, I spend forty minutes walking. In the summer, down at the waterfront. In the winter, it's up and down our very long corridors.

After lunch there are activities in the rec room or I enjoy some Newfoundland music, reading, or writing in my room. Dinner is early, and after eating it's my Newfoundland news time followed by game shows, or baseball, football, or hockey, as appropriate to the season. And then for me it's off to bed around ten.

Chapter Eleven

Changes

I have so many pleasant memories that I can't hope to cover them all in this book. Growing up in Rose Blanche was an experience I wouldn't trade for anywhere else I've seen or read about. We might have been out of touch with many of the things in our modern world, and we didn't have many of the materialistic accoutrement that people have today, but we lived well. I had enough to provide me with a very enjoyable childhood. Since just about everyone in the community was in the same boat, as it were, we didn't spend much time worrying about things we didn't have. We just made the most out of the things we did have. There may have been many things I had to cope with later, when I got out into the world, but I always felt that my growing up in Rose Blanche prepared me well.

Things have changed from the way it was when I grew up in the nineteen thirties and forties, but whenever I come to Rose Blanche, even if it's for only a few days, it seems like I am still living my dream. I take great pleasure walking down the road. It's paved now but it follows the same route it did back then. I like to sit for a while on the same rock or lean on the rails where the men gathered in the evening and discussed everything—starting with the weather and then progressing to what was in the news and even sometimes politics.

I can close my eyes and see and hear Uncle Israel talking about the way it was when he was a boy growing up. He wondered what the world was coming to, the ways things were changing. What he would think if he was alive now! I can see, in my mind's eye, the many men and women, most long passed away now, as they walked up and down the road. I can still see the fishing boats, the seemingly everlasting fog, and hear the loud claps of thunder echoing off the rocks.

No matter how hard conditions were in those days, there was always the hope that things would get better. That dream was inspirational and even today, when I go home to Rose Blanche, I am infused with a new dose of hope for the future. A visit home is like a new spring tonic.

We are largely the result of our heritage. What we are and what we will become in the future to a large extent is determined by what has gone on before in our lives. The way of living, the value system, the teachings of our parents and elders, influence our own thinking and our current outlook and way of life. For my children and grandchildren, this is some of what went on before, and shapes who you are and who will become. I honestly believe that I am who I am mostly because of my growing up in Rose Blanche.

The poet John Donne said that no man is an island unto himself. I give thanks, credit, and a whole lot of appreciation for the support, inspiration, and moral base that I was ingrained with from my loving parents, my church, my school, my students, my fellow army officers, my wife and daughters, the

Newfoundland outports of my early teaching attempts, and the whole community of caring and good people of Rose Blanche.

George Rose.

www.ingramcontent.com/pod-product-compliance
Lightning Source LLC
Chambersburg PA
CBHW060833120626
46557CB00001B/485